OK

# ALL-TERRAIN ADVENTURE VEHICLES

*Also by John Malo:*

CANOEING

MALO'S COMPLETE GUIDE TO
CANOEING AND CANOE-CAMPING

WILDERNESS CANOEING

SNOWMOBILING: THE GUIDE

# All-Terrain Adventure Vehicles

## BY JOHN W. MALO

*The Macmillan Company, New York, New York*

*Collier-Macmillan Limited, London*

The Macmillan Company
866 Third Avenue, New York, N.Y. 10022
Collier-Macmillan Canada Ltd., Toronto, Ontario
Library of Congress Catalog Card Number: 70-187074

FIRST PRINTING

Printed in the United States of America

*TO ALL PRESENT, AND FUTURE, OWNERS OF RECREATION VEHICLES:* may your days afield be filled with joyful and purposeful activity—but never at the expense of your fellow man, lesser creatures, the soil, woods or water.

# CONTENTS

# INTRODUCTION

FEW, if any, natural domains deny access to modern day man. Roadless areas, far-flung, out-of-the-way places, and rugged land, where a potential for adventure exists, can be explored and enjoyed today as never before. Through the imaginative creation of varied vehicles, individual interest and energy, and a wandering dream, man is able to probe remote corners of his world.

The array of off-road vehicles spurs the imagination, for transportation history is being made by this new variety of runabouts. They are available in many forms, a part of the booming recreation outlook that extends man's experiential field to bounds never before dreamed of, or believed attainable. Neither sand nor snow, mud nor marsh, offers an obstacle for the adventurer with a suitable vehicle. The varied off-road creations enable the user to probe once inaccessible places and to experience the exhilaration of challenging new worlds, with new dimensions in texture, tempo, climate, and color.

There is a broad selection of vehicles for the recreationist and sportsman, who are going beyond the two-car stage into many-vehicle ownership. The basic factors underlying the growth of off-road aficionados are many: increasing leisure, ennui, retreat from urbanization, etc. Americans spend an estimated 150 billion dollars annually in pursuit of various pleasures. Of course, liquor consumption, movie going, and night clubbing are included in this statistic, but a large share is spent by outdoor activists who offer their pleasure dollar for pursuits on land and water with vehicles and craft.

The purchase of a change-of-pace vehicle presupposes adequate leisure in which to use it. The outlook for increased free time in the near future reads like something out of Utopia. Four days of work, then three days of rest is gaining the approval, more and more, of employers and employees— representing one area where labor and management agree. Never before in man's history will such an abundance of leisure have been available, but sociologists agree that the increased freedom from working schedules carries with it a responsibility—to find suitable projects for man's energies, satisfactions, and aggressions.

As a consequence of the short work week, the trend toward a second home, a retreat in the country, mountains, or seashore, seems likely to burgeon. Over 2 million U.S. families now have second homes, and added to that figure, are thousands of varied recreational vehicles, houseboats, small cabins, and abodes, that do not qualify statistically as permanent homes. FHA mortgages on second homes (up to $18,000) will soon be available. Authority for this was approved by Congress in 1968, and the seasonal home will no longer have to be winterized or meet the rigid requirements of permanent homes to qualify.

Most second homes are located near water with beaches and marinas, in ski country, or near golf courses, tennis courts, bridle paths, forests, lakes, etc., which offer breathing space, a slower tempo of living, and a way of life that adds up to enjoyment for all members of the family.

It is an indication of resourcefulness and imagination when a family takes advantage of all that their environment has to offer—when it relates its leisure time activity to locale. Such families will use the dune buggy on long stretches of beach and sand dunes, the four-wheel drive vehicle on deep wood and mountain trails, the airboat in swamp and sawgrass country, the inflatable raft on wild rivers, the trailbike on wilderness paths, and snowmobiles in the snowbelt. This marriage of vehicle to locale is what this book is all about.

The sportsman and his family in the market for a recreation vehicle are able to select from a wide range of specialized machines for experiencing their backyard environment and beyond. Good luck with your type of magic carpet transportation, and as good fortune comes mostly to those who are prepared for it, perhaps this book can help.

# PART I

# All-Terrain Vehicles

## 1. THE GO-ANYWHERE MACHINES

The most ingenious of motorized carriers are the all-terrain vehicles, commonly referred to as ATVs, which climb like mountain goats, float on water, slosh through mud, churn through swamps, and ride over sand.

Invented in Canada more than a decade ago, there are now more than 50,000 of these odd-looking, go-anywhere vehicles performing amazingly by carrying recreationists beyond the pavement and crowds and aiding those in professions, trades, and services that require outdoor transportation.

### DEFINITION OF AN ATV

"Six fat tires on a bathtub," is one facetious driver's reference to it. "All-terrain vehicles," aptly says Roy Maddox, of Mobility Unlimited, "are probably best described as designed for off-road operation and capable of traversing rough or otherwise rough terrain during virtually all ground conditions in any season."

The geographical usefulness of the ATV encompasses that of a snowmobile, the dune buggy, and the trailbike by not only being able to go wherever they dare go, but also to roam beyond —at speeds on land up to 35 miles per hour (mph) for the average vehicle, and on water a speed of 2 to 4 mph. With attached outboard motor or marine jet propulsion unit, an ATV can achieve 10 mph as a watercraft, but to avoid trouble, the driver dare not venture on other than calm water with little current and no wind. The spinning, ribbed tires of the water-borne ATV propel the vehicle with limited stability and maneuverability. Some states require that ATVs be registered as inboard motorboats, equipped with running lights, fog whistle or horn, and fire extinguisher.

### TYPES OF ATVS

"All-terrain vehicle" is an all-inclusive term, and in a sense, certain dune buggies, the three-wheel bike, and the swamp buggy qualify as ATVs, for they too are able to negotiate multiple types of terrain.

Manufacturers have designed three general groups of true ATVs.

1. Most ATVs consist of a one-piece body with multiple wheels, the most popular being the 6-wheeler, accounting for approximately 90 percent of those in use during the early 1970s. This one-piece body type is characterized by its dependence on soft, squishy, low-pressure tires (2 to 4 on each side), which supply both suspension and flotation. There is no need for springs, since the balloon tires bounce off obstacles, providing

a smooth ride. Although not all of the tires touch the ground at any given moment, those that do furnish suitable traction. The buoyancy of the large tires, which keep spinning in water, gives paddle-wheel-like propulsion.

2. Some ATVs have an articulated body consisting of two independent watertight hulls capable of twisting opposite to each other in response to terrain conditions with all wheels constantly in contact with the ground.

3. The third type of ATV uses army-tank-type rubber tracks that run over wheels in continuous action, applying less ground pressure per square inch and giving improved mobility in soft ground or snow. Some manufacturers with wheeled ATVs offer the option of adding tracks which fit over the wheels.

The types of terrain over which you will do most of your driving should determine which type of ATV is best for you.

**Weight and Size** The smallest ATVs, used strictly for recreational purposes, weigh from 450 to 500 pounds, range in size from 82 to 87 inches (") and are capable of handling about 500 pounds of cargo and passenger weight combined.

The intermediate type of ATVs, for both recreation and service uses, weigh up to 1,000 pounds, and are capable of handling four passengers and a 1,000 pound cargo.

The larger, heavier models, designed for com-

*This Chaparal illustrates the most popular ATV type—the 6-wheeler.*

mercial and service uses, weigh up to 1,900 pounds, and are capable of handling 1,500 pounds of cargo. They range up to 97" in length.

## BODY, CONSTRUCTION, AND PARTS

The owner's manual that comes with the purchase of an ATV includes information on the engine, fuel mixture, starting, controls, and general operation, as well as maintenance. The manual should be read from cover to cover since it is important to be familiar with the working parts and controls, as well as maintenance and care, to obtain peak performance and trouble-free operation.

**Body** Construction, materials, and style vary greatly among models. One construction method consists of bolting all mechanical components to a steel frame, then fastening the frame within the body. Another method requires attaching all the individual components directly to the fiberglass or vacuum-formed plastic body. Most of the styled bodies are brightly painted, lightweight, with high-impact thermoplastic, such as ABS, which is vacuum-formed, utilizing heat, pressure, and intricate forms.

The large, commercial-type models have metal bodies. In some, a combination is used—a steel chassis supporting the composition body. Engines range from 2 to 4-cycle, and from 8 to

35 horsepower (hp). Among the 2-cycle engines are the Rockwell JLO, Hirth, Sachs, Kohler, and Canadian Curtiss-Wright. Among the 4-cycle engines are the Tecumseh, Briggs and Stratton, Wisconsin, Ford V-4, Wankle, and Volkswagen.

**Drive Power** Most machines transmit power with variable clutches, which shift automatically. Acceleration is by a twist or squeeze on the handlebar throttle or a push on the joy stick in the direction the driver chooses to go. He pushes forward to speed up, and backward to shift into reverse.

**Brakes** Hydraulically operated disc brakes are used on most models, and some brake by a shift into reverse.

**Controls** There is a great variety of types of control. Many ATV drivers prefer the steering wheel and foot throttle to approximate the driving of an automobile. Most models include the post and hand levers for throttling and braking. Steering an ATV is a new experience to most drivers, as in the majority of models turning requires braking on one side while accelerating on the other to bring the vehicle around.

**Tires** Probably the most important, and the best identifying feature of an ATV is the low-pressure (1.5 to 2 pounds pressure per square

ABOVE: *The flexing ability of ATV tires conforming to an irregular surface*

BELOW: *A Max being backed off a traveling trailer*

## SPECIFICATIONS

| Illus. No. | Description |
|---|---|
| 1 | Gas Cap |
| 2 | Gas Tank 3 gallons |
| 3 | Headlight |
| 4 | Headlight Rim |
| 5 | Front Floor Pan |
| 6 | Top Frame |
| 7 | Power Pack Frame |
| 8 | Middle Axle |
| 9 | Sprocket Assy |

## SPECIFICATIONS

| Illus. No. | Description |
|---|---|
| 10 | { #40 Chain 124 links |
|  |   #40 Chain 76 links |
|  |   #40 Chain 51 links |
| 11 | Hub |
| 12 | Rear Axle |
| 13 | (same as front) |
| 14 | Lower Body |
| 15 | Rubber Bumper |
| 16 | Lower Frame |
| 17 | Upper Body |
| 18 | Rear Tray |
| 19 | Rear Screen |
| 20 | Muffler |
| 21 | Flexible Exhaust Pipe |
| 22 | Battery Box |

## SPECIFICATIONS

| Illus. No. | Description |
|---|---|
| 23 | Motor |
| 24 | Choke |
| 25 | Front Seat |
| 26 | Dash Handle |
| 27 | Accelerator Grip |
| 28 | R.H. Steering Lever |
| 29 | L.H. Steering Lever |
| 30 | L.H. Steering Grip |

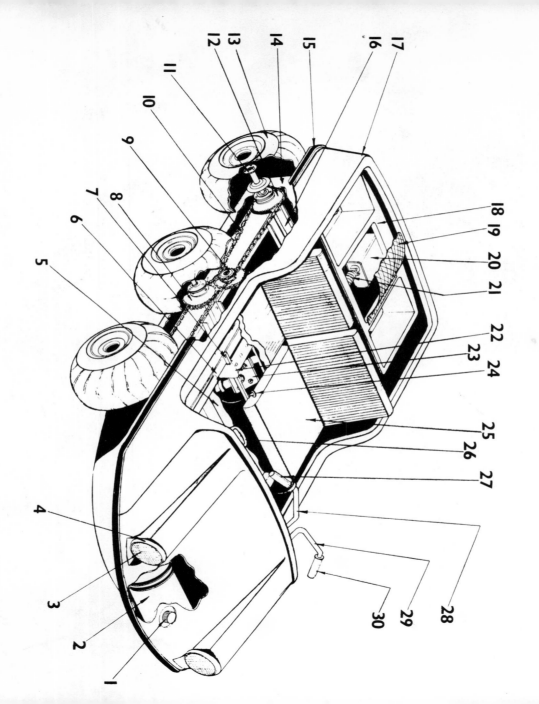

## BODY ASSEMBLY

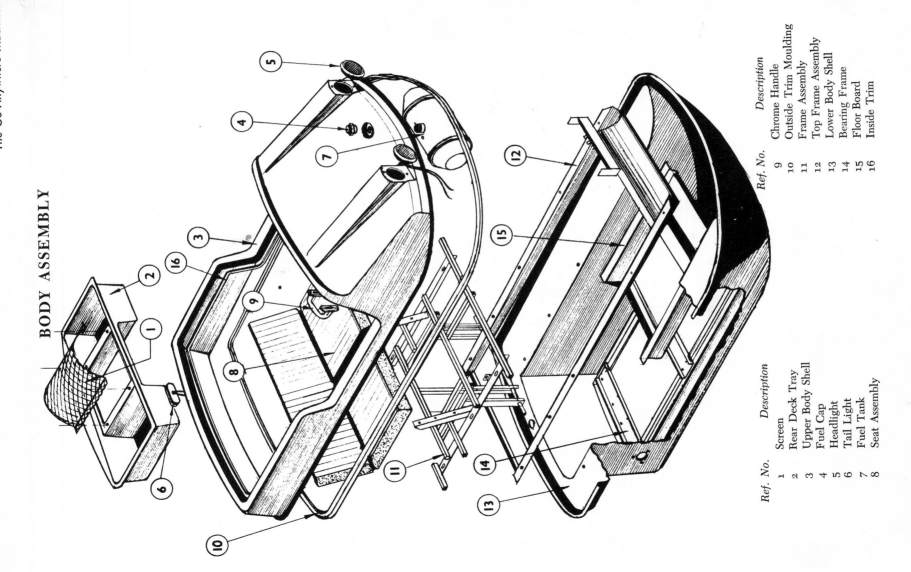

| Ref. No. | Description |
|---|---|
| 1 | Screen |
| 2 | Rear Deck Tray |
| 3 | Upper Body Shell |
| 4 | Fuel Cap |
| 5 | Headlight |
| 6 | Tail Light |
| 7 | Fuel Tank |
| 8 | Seat Assembly |

| Ref. No. | Description |
|---|---|
| 9 | Chrome Handle |
| 10 | Outside Trim Moulding |
| 11 | Frame Assembly |
| 12 | Top Frame Assembly |
| 13 | Lower Body Shell |
| 14 | Bearing Frame |
| 15 | Floor Board |
| 16 | Inside Trim |

# SERVICE MANUAL

## McKee Roughrider

## SAFETY PRECAUTIONS

1. Do not operate vehicle in a closed building unless you pipe out the exhaust fumes.
2. Make sure hands and clothing are at a safe distance from all movable parts before starting.
3. Never run vehicle without front floor pan.
4. Do not add fuel with engine running. Always shut the engine off and allow for cooling if possible.
5. Do not over-fill gas tank. Leakage around cap may occur when operating over rough terrain or on a steep incline.
6. Always remove key from ignition switch when vehicle is parked.
7. Always check vehicle for gas leakage before smoking.
8. Make sure ignition switch is in "off" position before working on vehicle. Best results is to remove key.

## ENGINE AND ACCESSORIES

Your McKee all terrain vehicle is equipped with a JLO Model 230, two-cycle engine, 14 h.p. at 5000 r.p.m. Maximum ground speed at 5000 r.p.m. is 30 m.p.h.

The exhaust system is connected by a flexible pipe. The muffler is mounted at the rear of the vehicle.

A see-through fuel tank is located at the front of the vehicle.

The engine generator provides 12 volts, 40 watts. A key switch on the dash is used for starting the vehicle and is also the switch for the lights.

## REPAIR BODY — FIBERGLASS

1. Be sure that the body is dry and clean where it is to be repaired.
2. (a) Where necessary cut back fractured material to sound part of the body.
   (b) Feather the hole, remove all paint and residue from area which patch will contact.
   (c) Where necessary form a suitable backing on which to build up new material.
3. Cut glass fabric or mat to shape and place on cellophane.
4. Prepare and activate, only enough resin to take care of a given patch.
5. Distribute the activated resin over the area of mat. Place another sheet of cellophane on top and with a blunt spreader squeegy the resin thoroughly through the mat being careful to work out all air entrapments.
6. Paint the area to be prepared with resin and put the patch in place. With your hands and the spreader, form the mat through the cellophane firmly into all contours.
7. After the resin has set, you may remove the cellophane, not before. Rough sand shiny surface before applying next patch.
8. After enough material has been laminated to re-establish the original thickness of the section, you are ready to sand and finish.

## LUBRICATION

Normally the McKee all terrain vehicle requires no lubrication. All bearings are sealed etc. However, as the machine is amphibious, it will hold water if left out in the rain. Be sure and drain machine on a steep incline for better drainage. Grease chains if machine has been used with water trapped in bottom.

## FUEL MIXTURE

Your McKee all terrain vehicle is equipped with a JLO Model 230 engine. This engine gets its lubricant from the fuel. Use a good grade two-cycle engine oil for best results: **Never** use ordinary auto engine oil. We recommend Bardal VBA or Castrol Super Two Stroke Oil, using a 40 to 1 mix. If using a 20 to 1 mix, the high speed jet on the engine carburetor must be set richer to allow the heavier mixture to flow.

## TOO MUCH FUEL

Open choke and throttle completely. Turn the engine over a few times. If engine still does not start, remove spark plug and turn engine several times. Now replace spark plug and start engine.

## NO FUEL

Check whether carburetor or fuel lines are plugged. Clean filter screen at carburetor, fuel line and fuel strainer.

## ENGINE RUNS UNEVENLY OR CEASES TO RUN

Spark plug is fouled or carburetor setting is too rich.

## ENGINE CONTINUES RUNNING ALTHOUGH SWITCHED OFF

1. Carburetor setting is too lean (re-adjust).
2. Heat value of spark plug is too low (use plug with higher heat value).

## Changing Tires

Elevate machine to clear tire from ground. Loosen and remove three lock nuts holding tire to hub and pull off (tool necessary is a one-half-inch socket, 6" extension).

## Brake Adjustment

Tighten bolt "B" to the point where the rocker bar can be sprung back to leave a ⅛" opening at "C" while the brake band is clamped tight. Do not set bolt too tight as this will decrease efficiency.

After rocker bar is properly adjusted, set jam nuts on brake rod "D" so that there is 1/16" clearance at "E" with rocker bar in position shown by dotted lines.

**Note:** The brakes will require adjustment after first few hours use.

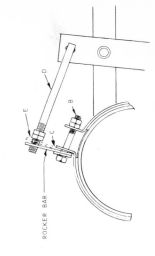

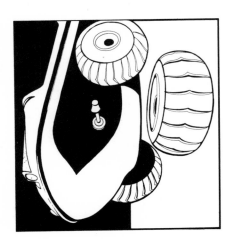

inch) balloon tire, furnishing the flex that is necessary to grip irregular and soft surfaces with a wide track-print that is easy on the terrain. On most models, the flexible tires give a cushioning effect, and serve as the suspension system. They actually can roll over a person without injuring him, proof that the machines can operate on delicate surfaces, such as lawns and golf courses—even in the radish patch.

**Axles** Axles range in diameter from 1" to 1.25" and are heat-treated. The smaller diameter axles, when broken or bent, can be replaced in 15 minutes. The larger axles require a complete disassembly and cannot be replaced in off-road locations.

**Center of Gravity** The low center of gravity makes the ATV very stable on steep-pitched slopes up to 45 degrees (°), and fairly seaworthy when afloat. During amphibious travel,

for safety, the freeboard, when the craft is fully loaded, should approach 15". Drivers and passengers will discover that although there is adequate stability in most ATVs, the open cockpit, low sides, shallow hull, and absence of hand-holds create the danger of tumbling out when climbing steep grades.

**Trailering** The ATV is not road licensable and must be towed or trailered for use away from home. Most models fit into the bed of a pickup truck or on trailers made especially for the model by the manufacturer.

### GENERAL MAINTENANCE

**Engine** The 2 or 4-cycle engine that propels most ATVs represents a sensitive mechanism that, when properly used, lubricated, and maintained, will purr for many trouble-free miles. It will not, however, function to its optimum level when abused. The most expensive engine will not perform efficiently, even with only 1 or 2 of the following: fouled, damaged, or incorrectly-gapped spark plugs; a dirty carburetor; clogged filters; plugged gas line; loose battery cables; low-grade gas or improper fuel mixture; loose wire connections; improper ignition timing; or a slipping clutch. Constant watchfulness of the various systems of your ATV is a must. You do not have to be a mechanic to apply preventive measures and care.

**Lubrication** Essential too, is the lubrication of all moving parts: roller chains, sprockets, clutch, roller bearings, axles, chain links, etc. Grease and oil prevent wear to metal and damage to moving parts, and save the owner a lot of money in part replacement and repair.

**Other Checks** The condition of all controls and gauges, lights, battery, tire pressure, and body should be checked before use.

**Storage** During periods of non-use, store the vehicle according to the owner's manual. It is not necessary to drain the gas tank since the addition of a stabilizer eliminates the corrosive actions of varnish and gum, and inhibits the breakdown of gasoline.

A lot of research went into the creation of the

## REPLACE MASTER LINK ASSEMBLY

1. Slide the lock off the master link "A".
2. Remove the connector plate "B".
3. Pull out the master link "C".

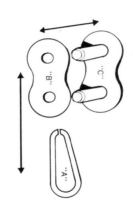

## AIR FILTER

The air filter located on the top of the carburetor should be checked after every 25 hours of operating depending on the circumstances under which the vehicle is used. If the filter is clogged and is not changed, normal breathing is restricted causing serious wear and poor performance.

## TIRE MAINTENANCE

Tire pressure should be set at approximately 2 lbs. If a guage is not available, inflate the tire to a height of 20 inches. Do not over inflate as it will void the warranty of the tire manufacturer. Another method is to put a measuring tape around the tire and inflate to 62" circumference.

If a tire on one side of the vehicle is over-inflated, it will tend to veer in opposite direction requiring constant steering correction to maintain a straight course.

## REPAIRING TIRES

Depending on the size of cut, patching can be done by a bicycle patch or a tubeless tire plug.

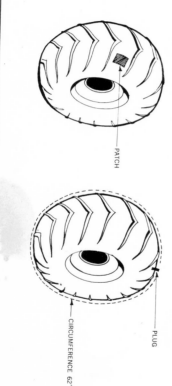

PATCH

CIRCUMFERENCE 62"

PLUG

ATV, and with the owner's cooperation and care, it is capable of giving years of dependable and trouble-free driving. Most companies guarantee their products for a certain period of time. The engine is usually guaranteed for a year.

The service manual offered by many companies is replete with technical data and intended to help mechanics resolve the various problems of engines, drive systems, ignition, body, tire repairs, etc. Some sections of the service manual for the McKee Roughrider are reproduced here, to show what manufacturers deem important to the proper operation and maintenance of their vehicles.

## CARBURETOR RE-ADJUSTMENT

Changing carburetor settings on two-cycle engines alters the amount of lubrication the engine receives. If adjustment is necessary, stop engine then turn idle fuel and main fuel adjustments all the way in until they bottom lightly. **Do not force closed.**

Tillotson Carburetor — Idle 1 turn open — Main 1½ turns open.
Walbro Carburetor — Idle ¾ turn open — Main 1 turn open.

Final adjustment is made with engine running at normal operating temperatures. Main Fuel adjustment may be leaned **slightly** for better performance. DO NOT RUN ENGINE AT "TOO LEAN A CARBURETOR SETTING."

## SPARK PLUG

Remove spark plug and check condition after every 25 hours of running. Replace plug if carbon fouled or has cracked porcelain. Do not sandblast, wire brush, scrape or otherwise service plug in poor condition. Best results are obtained with a new plug. Adjust spark plug gap to .020" and retighten spark plug to 27 foot lbs.

Bosch or Champion heat value according to operation conditions

| | L99 | L230 | L295 | L300 | L340 |
|---|---|---|---|---|---|
| Mainly at Medium Load | W175T1 L95Y | M240T1 K9 | M240T1 K9 | M240T1 K9 | M240T1 K9 |
| Mainly at full load | W225T1 L87Y | M240T1 K9 | M240T1 K9 | M280T31 K7 | M280T31 K7 |
| For racing | W240T1 L81Y L82Y | M280T31 K57R | M280T31 K57R | M310T31S K54R | M310T31S K54R |

## SPARKPLUG FACES

**WHITE COLOUR**
Spark Plug is too hot. Take plug with higher heat value.

**BLACK COLOUR**
Spark plug is too cold. Take plug with lower heat value. The right plug should be brown. Prior to changing plug, control carb. setting. The white colour of a spark plug can also be due to a too lean carb. setting.

**Note:**
To avoid spark plug fouling, do not let engine run at idling speed for a long time.

The Attex and a trailer-camper offer a portable rig to travel where game abounds.

# 2. SERVICE AND RECREATIONAL USES OF THE ATV

Versatility is demonstrated by the wide range of services the ATV performs. Manufacturers continually receive communications about new uses for their models.

Home owners hook up a blade attachment to the front of an ATV, and use it for clearing snow, towing a set of gang-reel mowers and trimming large yards and lots. Some attach trailers for hauling jobs.

To ranchers, resort owners, and camp directors, a heavy-duty ATV, with or without a trailer, offers more advantages than a horse. In all seasons, the vehicle is ideal for spreading seed and fertilizer; checking fences and gates; distributing feed and hay; spraying crops and orchards; and hauling fence posts, boats, outboard motors.

## SPECIFIC EXAMPLES OF ATV SERVICE USES

The Wisconsin Department of Natural Resources uses a Busse ATV for fire fighting and chemical spraying for the eradication of rough fish. The apparatus for fire fighting includes a 100-gallon tank and a self-contained portable pump and engine, which are effectively carried by the vehicle through rough and soft areas and may stop a fire before it gets out of control. The use of the Busse wagen on spraying projects en-

ables crews to get into almost inaccessible potholes and headwaters that were formerly reached only by helicopter. It is also used in a wild goose feeding program covering a 2,000-acre marsh.

The Roughrider recently supported a geophysical team on an electromagnetic survey on Bathurst Island in the Canadian Arctic region, 100 miles east of the magnetic North Pole. The scientists used the ATV to traverse and tote a cargo of instruments over barren tundra and desolate land.

The Attex is used to patrol the city beaches in Hollywood, Florida and Marine Corps lifeguards at Camp Pendleton, near San Clemente, California also use them. Family groups use the ATV as a floating raft for swimming, snorkeling, and fishing.

Every Alaskan male resident lives an outdoor life, and most are serious sportsmen. Much of the labor in hunting is characterized by packing man and gear 20 to 30 miles across muskeg or "jack brush" which grows in clumps on permafrost, becomes similar to a marsh when partially melted, and is like jello except in the coldest temperatures. The Trackster and other ATVs enable the "last frontier" hunter to get into the tundra with ease, to stalk game, and to pack it out—instead of hopping from clump to clump of unstable muskeg for long distances.

Conservationists accept only the ATVs with

large rubber tracks and low ground pressure which do not damage the delicate tundra. Heavier vehicles with metal tracks can cut through the muskeg and sever the exposed roots, causing permanent scars and starting erosion. The environment is a major concern with Alaskan conservationists, where the number of sportsmen with vehicles is increasing.

George X. Sand led the first ATV safari through Florida's vast Everglades—through Big Cypress Swamp to Marco Island on the Gulf of Mexico—to check the disrupting characteristics of the ATV. He found them to have little damaging effect.

Five men under the leadership of Jim Lytle, test-drove two Coots and gear in the ascent of 14,431-foot Mt. Elbert, the highest mountain in the Rockies. They achieved their goal—up steep inclines, through wooded areas, and above-timberline terrain consisting of barren rock faces and angular boulders—within 24 hours. Little disruption to the terrain was noted. As Lyle stated, "Sometimes we tried to retrace our route, but could not see where we had gone."

Tony Shiflet drove an Alsport Tracker on an Alaskan expedition that covered over 3,000 miles from Point Barrow to Seattle, Washington. The 19-day journey, completed in March, 1970 represented a victory for man and machine over rugged and merciless terrain.

Cowboys rounding up 400 stubborn beef cattle is not unusual, but when cowpokes at a Belle Glade, Florida ranch use ATVs (Terra-Tigers) in the roundup, that's news. After rainy weather, pastures become quagmires, and herding and driving cattle to a central penning area can be difficult for a horse. The mobility and the noise of an ATV keep cows on the move in an organized group. Hours of labor-saving efficiency are illustrated by one rancher who herded cattle in 20 minutes, a chore that formerly required 7 men on horseback 2½ hours.

The Chaparral ATV is serving the professional hunter in Lusaka, Zambia, a paradise in southern equatorial Africa. To facilitate safaris during the rainy season, which often makes hunting impossible, Ralph Rohwer, as well as copper mining prospectors, has turned to the ATV. In order to

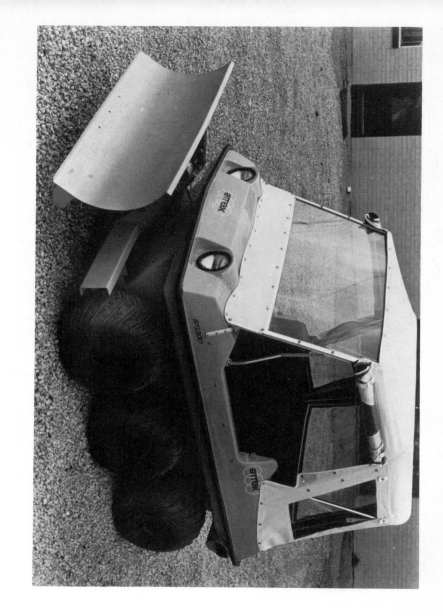

ABOVE: *Enjoying a shore lunch, after trolling for fish with the motor-rigged Argo*

BELOW: *The Roughrider hidden in the cattails offers an effective blind for duck shooters.*

OPPOSITE: *A blade attachment represents the easy way to shovel snow.*

bag trophy game in the remote back-country of Africa, where a breakdown could mean disaster, it is imperative to use a dependable vehicle. The ATV, as well as the four-wheel drive (4-WD) vehicle, meets all the requirements set down by the forbidding African bush.

"I can't believe that we've had so few fatalities in the area," said the sheriff of Lincoln, Nebraska. On two January days the mercury had dropped to 19° below, accompanied by gusts of wind up to 59 mph, and 14 inches of new snow. A dozen Cushman Trackster owners volunteered for rescue duty, and prevented any loss of life. Many volunteers spent up to 16 hours carrying 440 motorists, stranded in 6-foot drifts, to the safety of a truck stop; there they were housed and fed as 3 women started labor and 250 fairly serious cases of frostbite were counted. The expectant mothers were transported to the hospital, where one gave birth 4 minutes after arrival. It was conceded by rescuers and rescued alike that the track vehicles were the only motor vehicles that were able to move through drifts created by a wind that included 59 mph gusts.

Hunting guides in the Rocky Mountains and in Alaska take customers close to game without spooking the animals.

Mothers drive their children to school when snows prevent the school bus from reaching their homes.

A realtor in Minnesota drives prospective customers to remote cabin sites.

A power line service superintendent for the Black Hills Power and Light Company and his crew inspect every pole in the Rapid City, South Dakota district. The Trackster carries the inspection and repair crews across ranch land, bogs, high grass, and weeds.

Police departments in Lincoln, Nebraska; Roseburg, Oregon; and Carmel-by-the-Sea, California use ATVs in rescue and evacuation missions.

In Winter Park, Colorado, the ski area supervisor uses ATVs because of their ability to haul men, in a hurry, when a broken ski lift demands immediate attention. In the Sheltered Valley Ski Area, Wisconsin, the Trackster is used to groom the ski slopes: packing down new snow and breaking up icy crusts. The Mt. Peter Ski Area, near Warwick, New York, uses the Cushman machine in administering first-aid at the site of injury and for evacuating injured skiers. The machine is also driven to steep terrain where its snow-making nozzle is pointed at the correct angle to place the snow where needed.

The Amphicat scoots over sand, snow or water to serve fishermen, hunters, campers or explorers, and their gear almost anywhere they want to go. The missions have been unique: rounding up an alligator which escaped from a

*ABOVE: On any stretch of sand, the Max is able to rove at will.*

*BELOW: The ATV is an ideal hunting partner on any continent.*

zoo, hauling in the head of a dead whale to a game biologist for study, and transporting movie actors to shooting locations in remote places.

One illustration of the utility value of the Hustler ATV is indicated by its use for electric line inspection and minor repair work for the Arkansas Electric Corporation. Formerly, inspection of the line in swampy, hilly, and wooded areas required three days work using boats and jeeps. The Hustler does the job in one day.

Farmers benefit from the practically unlimited usefulness of a reliable ATV, including such services as checking the spread for erosion and gullies; herding cattle and sheep; hauling feed to stranded stock in stormy weather; reaching that new-born calf or colt in the back forty; gathering soil samples; checking crops for bugs, blight, and weeds; and clearing the snow from the driveway and out to the barns by attaching snow grader blades. Formerly, these chores had to wait until the terrain was dry. With the ATV, the farmer can move in any season without

rutting muddy fields or tearing up soft sod. A young person welcomes the challenge of responsibilities requiring the use of an ATV. When all the chores are finished, the same vehicle transports the workers to the backcountry for rewarding fishing, hunting, or touring—indicating that the ATV offers an interesting blend of work and play advantages.

## RECREATIONAL USES OF THE ATV

Besides service uses, the ATV is capable of reaching off-road areas for many recreational activities and fun projects: hunting, bird watching, exploring, prospecting, camping, picnicking, and rockhounding.

On ocean (as well as the Great Lakes) beaches where water, sand, soil, and marsh deter other vehicles, the ATV is able to rove at will. This is also true of the sand and stone expanse of the mountains and the desert lands of the Far West. Since the ATV, pressed to its maximum speed,

*In some snow-blizzard conditions, the track ATVs are the only motor vehicles that can get through deep drifts.*

offers a bumpy, hang-on ride, recreational value and safety come from a leisurely speed, which enables the driver to control the vehicle and the passengers to see more, while the soil is disturbed less.

Some specific hints for the ATVer include: en route to the campsite, climb or descend steep inclines with reasonable speed. And it's not cowardly to stop the vehicle and walk ahead to scout out a tricky contour in terrain. Constantly check on passengers and cargo when on bouncy roads. Carry a tool kit that contains the proper wrenches, screwdrivers, and pliers. Carry also tire repair kit and pump, oil, spark plugs, spare belts (if used), and extra gas. Remember that gas consumption is figured in hours of running time, not mileage. An interesting diversion, difficult terrain, speed of travel, and many other factors may use up fuel faster than the advertised 10 hours on a 5-gallon tank. For a trip to remote areas consider the hand-operated winch, to pull the vehicle out should it get bogged down.

The big advantage of an ATV to the migratory fowl hunter is that he can traverse water, shoreline, and marsh in search of suitable cover and at the same time transport his gun, ammunition, decoys, and lunch. Once finding a suitable area, he can properly camouflage the vehicle, which serves as a high and dry blind as well as a retriever for downed birds. After the day's shoot, toting out his bag offers little problem.

As this book unfolds, the recreational potential of many vehicles will be discussed, and the reader will realize that most of the projects and procedures are applicable for use with his ATV.

*Fishing's better when the Terra Tiger takes you to a secluded campsite and hidden lake.*

## ASSOCIATIONS

Although the general public is not very much aware of the ATV, a fast-emerging manufacturers' association is in the process of scheduling a series of trade shows for glamorous exposure of the various offerings.

Local clubs with extensive programs are being promoted by dealers of various ATVs with the hope of increasing participation—and sales.

Two national associations for individuals and clubs schedule rallies and racing. Realizing that the "hang up" on speed has hurt the sale of other vehicles, the associations are minimizing racing as a gung-ho, dare-devil type of activity, concerning themselves more with aspects of legislation, development of trails and areas of use, self-policing by members, and stressing family, sportsman, and young people's recreational uses: cookouts, picnics, safaris, rallies, etc.

In 1971, the National All-Terrain Vehicle Association staged its Second Annual Summer National Show and Rally, and many member clubs have embarked on annual rallies. Among them are the organized groups in Big Bend, Wisconsin; Rushville, Indiana; Lake City, Minnesota; Ashtabula and Nelsonville, Ohio; Phoenix, Arizona; Dover and New Alexandria, Pennsylvania; and Troy, Pine Knob, Pontiac, Lapeer, and Deckerville, Michigan.

For further information contact: California Off-Road Vehicle Assoc., 8612 Boyson St., Downey, California, 90242.

National All-Terrain Vehicle Assoc., 342 Broad St., New Bethlehem, Pennsylvania, 16242.

# 3. THE ATV'S IMPACT ON ECOLOGY

This is the decade of concern for ecology: the relationships between living organisms and their environment. The disruptive forces that imperil ecology are made up of many small components and, in recent time, we have come to realize that the harmonious relationships of living things, soil, air, and water directly affect our way of life and possible survival. Throughout this book, the ecology-disrupting nature of certain vehicles will be discussed.

As a result of the public's increasing awareness of the multitudinous problems of our land, the role, as well as the status, of the ATV is being closely scrutinized. Many question whether or not the off-road mechanized vehicle can be compatible with the environment and its conservation.

The multiple problems of protecting the natural environment from further deterioration by all off-road vehicles are being discussed by public officials and conservationists—some of whom are petitioning legislative bodies for control, regulations, and sensible use.

One manufacturer predicts that within a decade, virtually every outdoorsman in the country will own an off-road vehicle. If this is true, the impact on the environment could be shattering. The very versatility of the ATVs, regardless of their number, makes conservationists shudder at the thought of thousands of vehicles driving through and crushing bird and animal habitats, shattering the peace in woodlands and meadows, tearing up the delicate growth of seaside and mountain slopes, and flattening stream banks and the lush vegetation of watery places.

For the average city-dweller, the swamp (marsh or bog) is probably the least known realm in nature. He sees it as a foul-smelling, muddy, impenetrable, and forbidding area of stagnant water that should be eliminated, and man has drained, bulldozed, and backfilled them, using his techniques and machinery to destroy completely the soft land and the wet places.

However, the swamp in nature's plan is a vital link in the ecological chain. It teems with life—aquatic, subaquatic, and terrestrial. Minnows and frogs feed on its insect larvae, larger fish eat the minnows and frogs, birds of prey and turtles eat the fish, and mammals keep alive upon all the forms of life within the food chain—birds, fish, frogs, crayfish, clams, etc. The swamp's role in nature, that of serving many forms of life, has been an ever-recurring and orderly pattern since the dawn of time.

The swamp also plays a vital role in water reception and retention, and in releasing it gradually when needed in times of drought. Its rampant, junglelike growth plays a vital role in the water-edge's values: furnishing a wildlife habitat, containing soil in times of flood, and slowing down sedimentation. On and on, the lessons of nature are preached and practiced—if undisturbed by man.

The strong plea of the author, combining his voice with those of kindred bent, is for the ATV driver, who has the power to destroy a redwing blackbird's nest woven in the cattails, fish roe that attaches itself to water weeds, and the mud bottom that serves as an incubator for insect larvae, to use the vehicle with discretion. Travel the prescribed paths. Don't unnecessarily smash one weed. If 20 ATVs left a lake or river via different routes, think of the destruction—it would be akin to a bulldozer running wildly over a crowded campsite.

Soil is most vulnerable to motorized vehicles, especially when the tires are spun at a high speed, causing damage to soil, living plants, and minute organisms. An ATV requires but a mere flick of the finger to spin its wheels, gouging a furrow in the firmest terrain.

Forest soil is layered: on top are composted leaves that cover the deeper organic matter (humus) which rests on the nearly pure mineral soil (pulverized rock). The top mat of decaying leaves prevents the lower layers from being disturbed or washed away. The action of bacteria (millions to a pound of soil) aids the assimilation of dead materials, fosters water-retention qualities, and bestows nutriments to the roots of growing plants for their healthy growth.

Gouging deep holes in woodland turf has many effects: the mixup of soil layers makes them more homogeneous, disrupts the bacterial action, and renders the nutriments useless. The compaction of soil by heavy vehicle pressure stops the air from penetrating the surface and aerating the soil. Another serious effect is that tearing away the upper protective layers lays bare the lower ones that can be washed away. As the disrupted soil is being washed downhill, it can act as a smothering agent to healthy soil in its path.

Trips afield with your ATV should be tempered with knowledge of the terrain conditions in the various seasons. Spring riding, especially on ground saturated with rain and melting snow, should be tempered with caution, as plant conditions are very dry and susceptible to abrasion and fire. A realization of your ability to do harm to the environment is the first step in keeping it to a minimum.

Federal officials of the Bureau of Interior, National Forests, and Bureau of Land Management, state conservation departments, and many civic groups are constantly conducting surveys, holding meetings and conferences, suggesting rules and legislation, and in many other ways attempting to cope with the ever-burgeoning problems of all off-road motorized activity. None have decreed or proposed the complete abolition of off-road travel. They try hard to accommodate all and to present a program suitable to most.

# 4. THE ARRAY OF ATV MODELS
## IN THE UNITED STATES
## AND CANADA

During the early 1960s, the ATV was practically unknown, but today there are more than 75,000 sloshing through swamps and skittering over various terrains.

In 1969, 6 major companies sold between 9,000 and 11,000 vehicles; in the following year, an estimated 30,000 units were sold, with increased competition from 12 new companies. The projection is for 40 more manufacturers to enter the field within the near future and Owens-Corning, manufacturer of fiberglass bodies used by many companies, projects a figure of 300,000 vehicles in use by 1976.

The models and manufacturers listed on the following pages serve as an introduction to the variety of vehicles that are available and indicates some designs of models in the future. Any company will be glad to send you literature and the names of their dealers in your area.

## BUYER'S GUIDE

In the parlance of vehicle owners there occur many abbreviations that are universally understood. Throughout the book the following shall be used:

| | |
|---|---|
| hp | horsepower |
| mph | miles per hour |
| cc | cubic centimeters |
| psi | per square inch (pressure) |
| " | inch (measurement) |
| ' | foot (measurement) |
| ° | degrees of measurement |

Such terms as: 2-cycle, 4-cycle, 2-speed, 12-volt, 13-gauge, 3-ply, etc. are obvious, and also shall be used.

(Note: The order in which the vehicles are listed does not imply preference or importance. They are listed in chronological order of visits and/or response to correspondence.)

**The Busse Wagen** (Busse Bros., Inc., Randolph, Wisconsin, 53956) is a well-researched and finely engineered 6-wheel, heavy-duty vehicle, featuring comfortable seating for 5 adults, a 40" x 54" luggage or cargo box, and 4 roll bars offering a lot of protection. It is designed to support passengers who wish to stand for sightseeing or for photography. A plexiglass windshield is standard, and curtains, which help retain the engine heat, are available for winter use so that below-zero travel can be comfortable.

On water, the vehicle has enough of a safety margin to carry a 1,000-pound load. The hull's strength comes from .125 aluminum—strong, but light enough to avoid using up the flotation capacity with dead weight. Chevron-tread design tires give a paddle wheel effect on water with controllability. The Wagen has been tested at spring flood time with passing grades on the Baraboo River, Wisconsin and on the Madison River in Montana.

Flotation on snow comes from a newly developed all-rubber and fabric track (a $400 option). The engine is Volkswagen with options of 4-speed manual, fully automatic, and 3-speed semi-automatic "stick shift," the favorite with customers.

The Wagen enables a family or group to get into the backcountry of marsh, mountains, desert, or woodlands. It is used also for conservation and warden services and for oil and mineral exploration work, as well as by resort owners, hunters, fishermen, photographers, and nature lovers.

Base price: including seats for 5 adults, semi-automatic transmission, acrylic windshield, roll bars, sealed beam headlamps, taillights, amperage meter, oil pressure gauge, fuel gauge, hour meter, and tachometer, $5,200.

Accessories: top and side curtains, $225; tonneau cover, $100; electric winch, $150; hand winch, $30; and trailer (2,500-pound capacity), $1,000. (Note: To eliminate a catalog effect, only a few of the accessory prices will be given. Please note that all prices quoted throughout the book *are approximate and subject to change without notice.*)

**The Cushman Trackster** (Jim Raglin Inc., 312 Anderson Bldg., Lincoln, Nebraska, 68508), known as a "twin-tracked, multi-purpose utility vehicle, built for tough work as well as for recreational purposes," is a separate breed in the ATV field. The Trackster evolved from extensive testing—first in the snowy and rocky country near Centennial, Wyoming, and then on Arizona desert sands and deep in Michigan and Oregon woods—prompting the manufacturer

to claim, "The Cushman Trackster is the most reliable all-terrain vehicle ever produced."

The Trackster runs on continuous tanklike tracks, powered individually and controlled by a T-handle for forward, turn, and back-up maneuverability coupled with a low center of gravity. The power plant is a 25 hp, 2-cycle, air-cooled, die cast engine. A 12-volt electrical system provides lights, starting, and charging for the standard automotive battery.

Top speed is 16 mph, gasoline capacity is 10 gallons, enough for an average day's operation. A parking brake allows the vehicle to be parked on difficult terrain.

The Trackster has a capacity of 800 pounds, and there is plenty of room for 2 people, plus auxiliary seating for 2 more. The vehicle is small enough to fit into the back of a pickup truck or on a small trailer. Total weight is 1,040 pounds.

Ease of control, traction and gradeability, and ample power are features that make the Trackster a unique vehicle that can easily negotiate 45° inclines, and in year-round use, traverse rocky, mountainous, wooded, sandy, snowy, or marshy terrain.

Dimensions: length, 92"; width, 62"; height, 41"; track width, 15½".

Price: including many specialized features, $2,880. Accessories: convertible cab with doors, $300; windshield, $44; windshield wiper, $8; rear seat cushions, pair, $24; skid plate, $36; radio suppression kit which squelches ignition noise for 2-way radio operation, $8. Also, specialized accessories for

snow removal, along with a trailer, $256; outboard motor bracket, $800; and others.

**The Amphicat** (Mobility Unlimited Inc., Box 100, Raymond, Mississippi, 39154) is heralded as "a different breed of cat." It is, indeed, a fast-running, agile cat. At the Spring, 1970 National ATV Rally in Traverse City, Michigan, a stock Amphicat in a field of 16 took the lead in the second lap and held there for the remaining laps. This bit of renown was foretold when, in 1968, the Amphicat won a Popular Mechanics award in the annual International Inventors and New Products Division.

Amphicat's pioneer status is authenticated by its creation as early as 1957 by a Canadian machinist, Ron Beehoo. "The world's first ATV", claims its present owner and manufacturer. "Unique best describes the Amphicat body, tires, transmission . . . all specially developed and completely different from

anything before. And its styling and exclusive componentry make it the most imitated ATV in the world", says the manufacturer.

Six tubeless, virtually puncture-proof tires provide almost unlimited mobility. They carry 1½ pounds of pressure, and although the vehicle weighs 480 pounds or more, ground pressure under the 6 tires is only 1 psi. The 2-cycle, air-cooled engine is controlled by a winterized throttle and choke, which powers the vehicle through a 3-speed (2 forward and 1 reverse) transmission, which is steerable in reverse.

Testing of the vehicle is an ongoing activity: during assembly, a dynometer run test; after the chassis has been placed in the body, a second test; then after complete assembly, a professional test driver takes the ATV on a 20-minute drive. Passing these tests, the Amphicat receives a general cleaning and new tires and is crated for shipment. Amphicats

*Trackster*

are warranted by the manufacturer to be free from defects and workmanship under normal use for a period of 90 days from the date of original purchase.

Price: 8 hp engine, $1,299; 16 hp engine, $1,599; and 19 hp engine, $1,645.

Accessories: fold-down, aluminum-framed windshield, $66; convertible top, roll-up side windows and aft curtains, $110; highway trailer, $208; trailer hitch, $15; fire extinguisher, $13; and many more.

**The Centipede** (Camel Co., 329 S. Central St., Knoxville, Tennessee, 37902) is a single entry in the field by a company with 50 years of dependable service in furnishing many leisure-time and camping products. The Centipede, an ATV with a well-tooled mechanical makeup, "won't require 4 hours of maintenance for an hour's worth of fun," claims the manufacturer.

Characteristics include a torque converter that never requires lubrication or adjusting, the nylon chain adjustment rollers virtually make the chain tension adjustment automatic, a Borg-Warner transmission providing a reverse gear, an electric starter, alternator which supplies a continuous source of power for the 12-volt sealed-beam headlights, 7-gallon fuel tank with gauge, and storage space on the rear deck for extra fuel and camping gear.

The Centipede has a carrying capacity of up to

600 pounds and is supported by 6 low-pressure tires (2 psi) which provide a soft floating ride. The heart of the vehicle is a North American Rockwell 19.5 JLO engine, which moves the Centipede across land and snow at 35 mph. And if you're on lake ice that's not quite thick enough, the vehicle will float.

Price: $1,495.

Accessories: a heavy-duty, all-steel recreational vehicle trailer, capable of carrying two snowmobiles, motorcycles, and of course, the Centipede.

**The Tracker** (Alsport Inc, 84 Whittlesey Ave.,

*Amphicat*

*Centipede*

ABOVE: *Chaparral*

BELOW: *Terra-Tiger*

Norwalk, Ohio, 44857) is both an ATV and a sporty snowmobile, where driver and passenger sit in bucket seats side by side in a convertible-sports-car-type of experience. The rakish design comes from a low-slung frame, recessed head and taillights, and wrap-around cockpit.

The Tracker gets its power from 24 to 38 hp Rockwell engine options, secured solidly on a heavy-duty frame. Propulsion comes from twin Polytrac Gates tracks; and control comes from an electric starter console stickshift, sports car steering wheel, forward, neutral, and reverse transmission.

For conversion into a snowmobile, the change from front tires to skis takes a few minutes, without requiring special tools, extra brackets, or fixture kits.

Three Tracker models are offered: 2/10 with 24 hp; GT-15 with 30 hp; and GT-15 Sportster with 38 hp. All models are 108" long, 51" wide, and 42" high. Tire size is 18 x 9.5 x 8, 2-ply tube type; fuel capacity is 6 gallons; load capacity is 500 pounds on land, 400 pounds on water; speed range is up to 65 mph on land, 5 mph on water.

Standard equipment includes electric starter, caliper disc brakes, dual head and taillights, automotive-type rack and pinion steering, rally steering wheel, console control gear selector, cigarette lighter, and others.

Price: 2/10 Standard model, $2,195; GT-15 model, $1,895; GT-15 Sportster, $2,395.

Accessories: cargo carrier, $22.50; tilt-bed hauling trailer, $259; skis or wheels, $84; rally pack kit: tachometer, speedometer, dash and console, $94.50; storage travel cover, $44.50; and others.

**Chaparral** (Chaparral Industries, 5995 N. Washington St., Denver, Colorado, 80216) has many features built into a beautifully contoured, cream-white Cycolac body: 6 wheels; 2 control handles; plenty of spunk from a JLO 20 hp engine; and Borg-Warner transmission that provides gear reduction, steering, braking, and reversing in a single, compact housing.

The vehicle seats 3 adults, or 2 adults and 2 children, making it an ideal family vehicle for beach touring, woods travel, rock hunting, gold panning, photographing, and picnicking.

Price: single-cylinder, 20 hp model, $1,695; twin-cylinder, 25 hp model, $1,795.

Accessories: convertible top, windshield, rear seat pad, trailer, hitch, camouflage cover, and regular cover.

**Terra-Tiger** (Allis Chalmers, Box 512, Milwaukee, Wisconsin, 53201), an early reliable in the ATV industry, is a swimmer, climber, snow-goer, hunting partner, and a fishing buddy.

The Terra-Tiger seats 2, carries a 600-pound pay-load, and provides 11 cubic feet of storage area for equipment. The model is powered by an 18 hp, 2-stroke, air-cooled engine that propels the 6 wheels at speeds up to 30 mph on land and up to 4 mph on water. A single steer tiller incorporates fingertip throttle and brake controls. A 10 hp engine model is also available. The electric starter, heavy-duty axles, and clutch are standard.

Across the land, the vehicle is used by outdoor enthusiasts in all seasons, as well as by construction crews, lumbermen, conservationists, beach patrols, and farmers.

Price: 18 hp model, $1,625; 10 hp model, $1,375. Accessories: a 300-pound tilt-bed trailer, complete with stop bar, tie-down chains, fenders, tail- and turn-lights, windshield, convertible top, and trans-port cover.

RIGHT: *Got'cha*

BELOW: *Coot*

**Got'cha** (Action-Age, Inc., 18780 Cranwood Parkway, Cleveland, Ohio, 44128) features fiberglass construction, foot pedal acceleration, hydraulic steering and brakes, electric starting, chromed hubcaps, and a gold finish with flakes of metal, in a sporty vehicle presentation for less than $1,000.

Got'cha is powered by an American-made 4-cycle, 8 hp engine, and the 4-WD and large flotation tires take it through snow, sand, surf, mud, brush, swamp, and water, and up grades as steep as 45°.

The jet-age-styled vehicle, with adjustable steering levers, and bucket seat, takes you to the fun at road's end.

Action-Age also manufacturers the Scrambler, a larger ATV which can carry a family of four.
Price: $995.

Accessories: headlight-taillight kit, chrome hubcaps, trim, and roll bar.

**Coot** (Cummings Engine Co., Inc., 10858 Harry Hines Blvd., Dallas, Texas, 75220), one of the originals in its type, has a small, amphibious, 4-WD, positive traction vehicle with 2 articulating steel hulls. It is powered by a 12 hp Tecumseh engine with two forward speeds and one reverse.

The Coot is small enough to be transported in a pickup truck, yet sturdy enough to carry a 1,000-pound load over land and a 600-pound load on water. It steps lighter than a walking man—5 psi compared to 7 psi for a man.
Price: $1,695.

Accessories: trailer, surrey top, roll bar, special tires, winch, outboard propeller, 4-wheel steering, and heavy equipment including: snowplow, 3-gang mower, sweeper, dump cart, and fertilizer spreader.

**The Attex** (ATV Manufacturing Co., 1215 William Flynn Highway, Route 8, Pittsburgh, Pennsylvania, 15116) ATVs include five models: the 208/TT with 8 hp engine; model 225 with 12.5 hp engine; model ST/300/D with 20 hp engine; model ST/340/R with 28 hp engine; and model ST/400/R, also with 28 hp engine.

The ATV Manufacturing Co. claims the Attex to be the most technologically advanced ATV available and that more families from Maine to Hawaii own their machines than any other. One of the early entries in the ATV industry, the development of Attex began in the fall of 1967. It sprang from humble beginnings, worked on first in an office building, then by stages, moving to one of the most modern manufacturing facilities in the country.

Today, the company manufactures just about every one of their component parts except the tires and engines. This independence from sub-contractors gives them control of the manufacturing process.

The Attex models include a transmission that utilizes 3 sets of planetary gears—one set for forward and reverse, the other 2 for steering, with gear-driven clutches activated by disc brakes. The body is of Royalite, an ABS thermoplastic of strength, durability, dimensional stability, and lightness. The tires of 11.5" x 20" size are Uniroyal, Firestone, or Goodyear. The axles are aircraft alloy, utilizing automotive ball bearings mounted outside the body for increased support.

Prices: model 208/TT, $955; model 225, $1,325; model ST/300/D, $1,595; model ST/340/R, $1,575; and model ST/400/R, $1,675.

Accessories: transport trailer with tilt-bed platform; camper-trailer that sleeps four; convertible fabric top; tonneau cover; trailer hitch; outboard motor bracket; rally pack which includes tachometer, speedometer, compass, roll bar, safety belts, rally stripes; and others.

**The Hustler** (Hustler Corp., Box 1283, Jonesboro, Arkansas, 72401), manufactured in a small, brother-

*Attex*

owned plant, uses 100 percent American-made components, eliminating the difficulty of obtaining parts and service. Its claim to fame is the Jacuzzi marine jet propulsion unit option ($250) that is capable of pushing the Hustler up to 10 mph, probably the fastest water speed of any ATV.

Besides having colors of tangerine and white or hunter green, Hustler's features include: neoprene motor mounts; a 5" duct hose that takes hot air from the block and the outside; and a dual power-tuned muffler, giving a 15 percent greater horsepower rating over straight pipe designs and enabling the

25 hp Canadian Curtiss-Wright, 2-cycle engine to push the machine and driver up to 35 mph—in reverse, as well as forward.

Other Hustler features include a total of 44 properly sealed ball, roller, and needle bearings; a steel frame with a fiberglass hull that gives a vibration-free ride; high traction from Goodyear balloon tires with 1½ pounds of air pressure; chrome hubcaps; hand-operated, dual-stick controls; rubber bumper; 4.7-gallon fuel tank; and sealed-beam rubber mounted headlights.

Price: $1,945.

Accessories: trailer, travel cover, windshield, cargo rack, rear set upholstery, tachometer, skid plate, and others.

Max (Recreatives, Inc., 30 French Road, Buffalo, New York, 14227) claims that the world doesn't stop when the seasons change; neither does the Max whether the fields are covered with clover or snow.

The 20 hp, 2-cycle JLO engine pushes Max up to 30 mph, and the Borg-Warner transmission combines in one integral unit, the functions of gear reduction, clutching, braking, and steering. Six axles

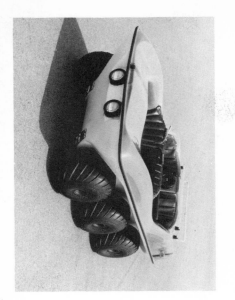

LEFT: *Hustler*
BELOW: *Max*

*MFX 4000*

with triple-sealed bearings never need lubrication. All of the above are structured around a heavy, 5" steel channel frame that keeps Max going on all types of terrain. The body is made of ABS thermoplastic with high-impact strength that cannot rust or rot.

Price, $1,545.

Accessories: trailer and hitch, convertible cab and doors, fold-down windshield, cover, roll bars, seat belts, and helmets.

**Mini-Skat** (Struck Corp., Cedarburg, Wisconsin, 53012) comes in kit form, enabling the do-it-yourself fan to enjoy an ATV with lower initial cost. The 6-wheeled Mini-Skat serves many purposes—for cross-country travel for camping and hunting, as a heavy-duty tractor for lawn and garden care, and as a general farm work vehicle. The Mini-Skat has a low-speed range of approximately 2½ mph for difficult cross-country travel. A secondary speed option of approximately 10 mph is available. The kit includes: a 7 hp Tecumseh engine, 6 tires 16" in diameter, with wide thread (16" x 7.50-8"), full-drive mechanism, seats, chains, sprockets, and all the necessary nuts, bolts, and screws.

Price: $398.95.

Accessories: electric start, $119.95; electric lights, $14.95.

**MFX 4000** (Massey-Ferguson Inc, 1901 Bell Ave., Des Moines, Iowa, 50315) is in the preliminary testing stage to determine feasibility of actual production of this unique recreation vehicle capable of operating on snow and water. Powered by a 55 hp Volkswagen engine, the MFX 4000 is designed to travel up to 55 mph on snow and 35 mph on water (fast enough to tow water skiers).

On snow, the amphibianlike craft operates on dual tracks with skis up front. For water travel, the operator simply removes the tracks and skis, and attaches a single propeller.

The vehicle has a fiberglass catamaran-type hull with a movable fiberglass simulated vinyl top and side curtains. The bucket seats have vinyl covering. Other features include carpeting, stereo tape player, heater, speedometer, tachometer, and hydraulic drive.

The MFX 4000 is 12' long and 5' wide, and weighs 1,200 pounds. It can carry 2 adults and 2 children.

Price: no price is quoted.

**TerraStar** (Lockheed Aircraft Service Co, Ontario International Airport, Ontario, California, 91761) is a possible entry into the ATV recreational field, after first serving in a specialized military capacity. Its unique propulsion system offers a new concept in ground mobility, capable of traveling the difficult terrains of the world: rice paddy, jungle, and tundra.

In this system, conventional wheels and tires are replaced by major-wheel assemblies. These assemblies include minor wheels mounted on secondary axles located radially about, and at some distance from, the major-wheel axle. The minor wheels carry wide-base, low-profile, low-pressure tires. A gear-train, housed in the hub with spokes on one side of the major-wheel assembly, transmits power to the minor wheels from a drive shaft carried through the tubular major-wheel axle.

Driving controls are uncomplicated: simple steering levers like those of a tracked vehicle; the usual brake, clutch, and accelerator; and conventional instruments. Control of the vehicle is accomplished by identical driver action on both land and water.

The model being developed for recreational use is by John and Robert Forsyth.

*TerraStar*

Price: recreational model, expected to retail for $2,000 to $2,500.

The Canadian ATVs represent heavy-duty, rugged pieces of equipment that are constructed to withstand a sometimes severe landscape. The major role of an ATV, that of negotiating difficult terrain, can signify much more above the border than it does in the United States. The Canadian vehicles adequately meet the challenge.

## BUYER'S GUIDE

**The Argo** (Ontario Drive and Gear Limited, 589 Fairway Road, Kitchener, Ontario, Canada) models come in 6 and 8-wheel styles with 28 hp, 2-cylinder, 2-cycle, air-cooled engine, which powers them over open ground at a 35 mph clip, and balloon tires.

The Argo 6 has ample room for 4 people or extra gear; the Argo 8 will carry up to 6 passengers or 1,000 pounds of gear, with excellent performance proven in cross-country, all-season operation in the Canadian North.

The high-impact plastic, orange-colored body, needs no further finishing. The front-mounted motor transfers power through a compact gear system and an automatic torque converter. There is a drive selector that offers reverse, neutral, low, and high settings.

An electric key start is standard, but a back-up manual recoil starter is provided. A see-through plastic fuel tank holds 5 imperial gallons (or, 6 regular gallons) of mixed oil and gas for approximately 6 to 8 hours of running time.

Price: Argo 6, $1,895; Argo 8, $2,295.

Accessories: trailer and hitch, windshield, convertible top, cargo cover, outboard motor bracket, two-wheel snow track, taillights, power winch, handrail, skid plate, snowplow and attachment, and heavy-duty tires.

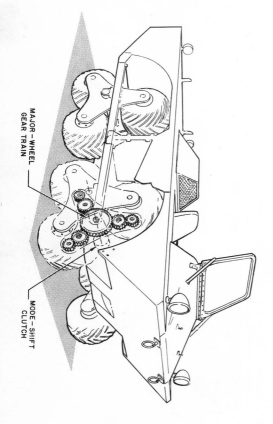

MAJOR-WHEEL GEAR TRAIN

MODE-SHIFT CLUTCH

RIGHT: *Argo*
BELOW: *Passe Par Tout*

**The Terra Jet** (Terra Jet, Inc., c.p./Box 724, Drummondville, p. que., Canada) is an ideal 4-season vehicle for the entire family. Nothing can stop it. Features of the 106" long, 55" wide, 850-pound, 4-wheel sport vehicle include 4-wheel drive; forward, neutral, and reverse transmission; automatic clutch; conventional steering; accelerator and brake pedals; and speeds of 45 mph on land and 5 mph on water with excellent stability.

The powerful 2-cylinder, 2-cycle, 28 hp engine enables the ATV to travel 45 mph (the maximum limit) on secondary roads in the Province of Quebec. The Terra Jet is used extensively for work on golf courses and baseball and football fields. Unique features include a roll bar, bucket seats, adjustable bumper, canvas top, and the motor belt which is claimed to be the strongest one on the market.

The warranty guarantees all new vehicles against any defect of materials and workmanship under normal use for 90 days.

Price: $1,695.

Accessories: many included as standard.

**The Passepartout** (Valcartier Industries Inc, Box 790, Courcelette, Quebec, Canada), known as P.P.T., was originally developed for rugged heavy-duty application in commercial and military environments, but its sporty design and easy maneuverability have won it popularity as a recreation vehicle. Women enjoy driving it especially because of its safe and easy handling characteristics.

The P.P.T. beautifully combines ruggedness and eye-appealing features: all-steel welded body on wide-set dual 3-ply nylon and rubber tracks, streamline design lines, and bright red color.

The P.P.T., in an on-going research program, is continuously being challenged in a severe testing and riding terrain, through swamp, wood, sand, snow, rocky ground, and steep hillsides. (Note: The P.P.T. is not a water traveling vehicle.)

Additional features include: a 22.5 hp Sachs engine; track width is 12", and track length is 196"; transmission with 2 speeds forward and 1 reverse; a 12-volt lighting system; and a 5-gallon tank capacity that gives 5 hours of running time. Its width of less than 4 feet enables the P.P.T. to be transported in any standard pickup truck or towed by automobile on a trailer. Engine options of higher hp are available.

Price: in the United States, $2,095, plus tax.

Accessories: tool kit and replacement parts, 12-volt battery, 45 amps, 75 watt, electric starter, and chrome hitch ball.

*Roughrider*

The Roughrider also features a fiberglass body which polishes up to a high lustre, eliminating sanding and repainting each season. Steering and braking throttle controls are on the handles, allowing plenty of seat and leg room.

The Roughrider's range of use includes the beaches of California, the rivers and lakes of Arkansas, the mountains and plains of the United States, the backcountry of Canada, the East and West Indies, and many other parts of the world.

Price: $1,495.

Accessories: trailer and hitch, waterproof canvas cover, reverse gear, and windshield.

**Roughrider** (McKee Bros. Ltd., Elmira, Ontario, Canada) stems from a production line of farm, industry, and home equipment, and has built into it many rugged construction features: a JLO model, 2-cycle engine generates 14 hp, capable of a ground speed of 30 mph, and ability to climb slopes up to 45°, and through bush, muskeg, snow, and sand in between. The power pack consists of engine, torque converter, and steering mechanism, all in one package. A service mechanic can remove the power pack from the machine in 15 minutes, facilitating easy access for cleaning or repair.

*Playcat*

**Playcat** (Playcat Industries, Inc., Box 39, Drummondville, Quebec, Canada) is a powerful all-purpose track-driven vehicle designed to master all types of terrain, except water. The body (length 97", width 50") is constructed of welded and molded aluminum with galvanized steel frame (18-gauge) and reinforced with steel plate in front (14-gauge). The 28 hp Kohler air-cooled engine drives the machine up to 30 mph both forward and in reverse. Traction in all seasons is supplied by one-piece endless rubber tracks, 13" wide, that run over 4 sets of 4 bogie wheels that give smooth suspension through their shock-absorbing qualities. The fixed "T" handlebar permits hand-operated accelerating and braking. Playcat vehicles are fully covered by a 90-day warranty on workmanship and materials provided by the manufacturer. In addition, the motor is guaranteed for a full year by its original manufacturer.

Price: $2,195.

Accessories: trailer, canvas cover, and cab enclosure.

# PART II

# Land-Roving Vehicles

# 5. THE FOUR-WHEEL DRIVE VEHICLE

The four-wheel drive (4-WD) vehicle, often called a jeep or jeep-type vehicle, offers great advantage to the owner who wishes to travel dirt roads, or for that matter, no roads at all. The 4-WD vehicle is what it claims—a drive at each or the four wheels so that if, on a tortuous road, three wheels are in the sky, the fourth will supply enough power to propel the vehicle and move it to a place where traction from the others can be supplied.

## HISTORY

The interesting forerunner of the present day 4-wheel drive vehicle is the army jeep. This ¼-ton capacity vehicle, capable of speeds up to 60 mph, came into prominence during World War II, where it served as a fast military reconnaissance car to replace the motorcycle. The spunky scatmobile represented the smallest vehicle (11′ x 4′) of the army's rolling stock.

The jeep served in all theaters of war with attributes of power, stamina, and maneuverability to whisk generals and key personnel to and from the battle zones; tow airplanes; and haul troops, small artillery pieces, ammunition, and other light cargo. The vehicle, with specialized fittings, also served as an ambulance, firefighting vehicle, mobile machine-gun mount, or radio patrol car. Its versatility and dependability prompted the noted war correspondent, Ernie Pyle, to remark, "Good Lord, I don't think we could continue the war without the jeep. It does everything."

The army jeep, however, was not without an objectionable feature: the vehicle lacked adequate ride cushioning, and traveling over bumpy terrain caused many a GI to suffer from fracture of the coccyx (tailbone).

Traveling the off-road domains is made to order for the modern offspring of the army jeep. It is ideally equipped with jumbo-size wheels with earth-gripping tires that roll over potholes, up hills, out of gulches, and through sand and mud. For these virtues, the jeep came into prominence again in the early 1950s. It was synonymous with the exciting uranium boom, when the Atomic Energy Commission was paying liberal sums for the ore. No other mineral, in the history of the world, had the political, defense, and fuel implications of uranium, the source for atomic power and nuclear energy. The trappings of the 20th century prospector, as he probed remote rock formations, included the jeep, pick, shovel, and the Geiger counter.

Today, the popularity of 4-WD vehicles, runs deep in the hearts of many men who used them in the army or on the backroads for exploration. Use of the vehicle for recreation came easily, and the present models are not topless or roughriding. Like every product in the automotive field, the 4-WD vehicle has become, without los-

*The 4-WD vehicle will see you through adventures beyond the pavement.*

*The 4-WD vehicle serves many people in many places.*

tear on the drive train, universal joints, and tires, while giving a smooth, quiet, and comfortable ride.

The 4-WD vehicle, besides serving ranchers, farmers, prospectors, forest rangers, gas station personnel, mailmen, salesmen, and school teachers, has become a second family car which mothers use for shopping and shuttling children to various activities. Families use them as one uses a station wagon, cruising the highways, keeping up with the traffic flow and then, off-road for recreational pursuits. On weekends and vacations, the 4-WD vehicle takes on its specialized role—adventuring beyond the pavement—and as an owner you'll be confident that come rain or snow, tidal wave or monsoon, mud-slide or hurricane, the vehicle will see you through.

As to costs, manufacturer's suggested retail prices, exclusive of state and local taxes, and dealer preparation charges, start at a base of $3,200. At the other end of the scale, a 6-passenger model with air conditioning, power brakes, automatic transmission, pleated vinyl trim, a V-8 engine, and polyglas white-wall tires can cost as much as $7,500.

In the past decade, 4-WD vehicles have increased by almost 500 percent and a high percentage of the sales went to buyers who indicated recreational use for the vehicle. Increasingly, the buyers come from the under 25 years of age group, who are mainly interested in the off-road capability of the 4-WD vehicle.

## SPECIFICATIONS

**Engine** In practically all models, there is a choice between a straight 6-cylinder (standard) and a V-8 (optional). The straight 6 engine, though not as powerful, offers an ecological

ing any of its off-road work-horse attributes, a stubby, but eye-appealing machine, with two-tone paint jobs, decorative dashboard, power steering, air conditioning, soft seats, and perhaps an AM-FM radio.

An important option is the set of free-wheeling hubs, which lock out the drive mechanism on the front axle and permit power in the conventional way (2-wheel drive). This saves gas, wear and

*The San Juan Mountains of southwestern Colorado, known as the "Switzerland of America," are a popular jeeping area.*

advantage in that you are less apt to spin the wheels and dig yourself into loose ground, and it is easier on gas consumption.

**Transmission** A 3-speed manual shift is standard, with 4-speed manual and 3-speed automatic as options. The gear transfer case offers high and low ranges for 4-WD and 2-wheel drive. A neutral position is provided for disengaging the engine's power and channeling it into another piece of equipment: mechanical winch, post hole auger, etc.

**Free-Wheeling Hubs** As indicated above, the hubs become free when disengaged from the power drive mechanism. They are also called "selective drive hubs." Their 2 positions, "lock" and "free," are set manually on the dial at the hub of each front wheel. Newer models can be set automatically from a dashboard switch.

**Skid Plate** The skid plate consists of a flat steel shield mounted underneath to protect the engine and vital parts: oil pan, oil filter, fuel and brake lines, gear linkage, and tie rods.

**Tires** Standard equipment generally includes 4-ply tubeless tires, but for the off-roader, tube tires, which you can repair in the field, are more advantageous. A heavy-cleated tire will be welcome in the back-country, but it will make vibration noise on the highway; a wide-tread tire gives better traction and support over loose sand and soil, but the increased surface in touch with the ground makes the vehicle harder to steer at slow speeds, and there are soil disrupting disadvantages. Weigh the alternatives before making a decision.

**Power Take-Off (PTO)** This is a highly specialized option which indicates the versatility of a 4-WD vehicle. With proper attachments, the PTO can be used to dig holes, pump water, run generators, and drill wells. Hydraulic winches, lifting devices, and snowplows are also used with the 4-WD vehicle.

**Wheelbase** The stubby dimensions of a 4-WD vehicle, wheelbase 90" to 100", give a bouncy ride, but the vehicle is highly maneuverable in rough country, and less apt to get "hung up" on boulders, logs, and crests of hills.

**Off-Road Equipment** For extended use in the back-country several items are offered: extra gas tank or jerry cans, tow chain, tool kit, shovel, first-aid kit, lamp or flashlight, and a mechanical or electrical winch, which enables the driver to pull the vehicle out of trouble, to pull timber off

*Colorado ghost towns and abandoned mining camps are best accessible by 4-WD vehicles.*

the road, to stretch barbed wire fencing, and to hoist loads.

## OFF-ROAD TRAVEL

The advantages of a dependable 4-WD vehicle to the hunter and fisherman are many; he can rove far from the paved road and concentrations of people, haul in all necessary equipment, including luxury items, use the vehicle as a base camp, roam the most likely looking areas, sleep in his vehicle at night, and with luck, take out his weighty game.

In some areas, the weekend 4-WD vehicle driver, whether he be an amateur or professional historian, can find great satisfaction in probing back-trails where the traces of the pioneer can still be found. The entire length of the Rocky Mountains is honeycombed with half-forgotten trails, abandoned gold, lead, copper, and silver mines, isolated cabins, and ghost towns.

These remnants stand as reminders of an age when mountain men, trappers, and missionaries first probed the unknown, hostile land. They opened it up for the hardy and hopeful prospectors, who, like ants, zigzagged nearly every mountain niche in their relentless search for precious ores. At the end of the 19th century, the gold and silver fever abated, and the land gave way to permanent settlers, farmers, and ranchers, as today it gives way to the recreationist.

The same fascination is true of the abandoned lumber camps in the northern tier of states, the forlorn coal mines, cemeteries, building sites, and many stretches of forgotten land in other states. Many of the evidences of a nostalgia-evoking past are there to be discovered and enjoyed, and with proper vehicle you can leave the solid highways, travel the time-faded trails, observe and relive some interesting and colorful periods in the opening up of our country.

The entire area of the Colorado Plateau in Colorado and Utah is laced with tens of thousands of miles of primitive land that is ideal for the 4-WD adventurer, and many of the miles are rarely used by vehicles, from month to month, year to year. Many of the grown-over roads were put there by the rugged and hardy miners making wagon ruts leading to their mines, to the waterhole, and toward town for supplies.

Almost 70 percent of the Colorado Plateau and adjacent New Mexico and Arizona is under the control of various federal agencies: Bureau of Land Management, Forest and Park Services, and the Bureau of Indian Affairs. The entire area is a fertile land for off-roaders to ply their hobbies: photography, rockhounding, prospecting, sketching, painting, geology, archeology, botany, and zoology.

## FAMILY PROJECT

Should you wish to close that generation gap with a hot-rodding son and a date-crazy daughter, try a 4-WD trek into the back-country with a definite project such as uranium prospecting, gold panning, rockhounding, or ghost town searching. Place the responsibility of the vehicle in the hot-rodder's hands, while the daughter tends to logistics, the horse or mule perhaps, the grub rations and menu, and you'll discover traits in your offspring you never before realized existed. The man-size challenges will be meaningful and real, and you'll find compatibility—even with a teenager.

## DRIVING IN ROADLESS AREAS

Before embarking on an extended trip to roadless areas, you must clear with the proper agency, whether it be a state or national park, public land, forest preserve, farmer, or rancher.

En route, first check the weather and stock up on litter bags. Include a 2-way repair light with flashing red beam, road-side reflectors or flares and an extra fan belt (in overheating situations

*Off-road equipment on this model includes all-weather top, winch, heavy-duty push bumper, and selective drive hubs.*

check this first, then the water level). Check the rear window view with equipment.

Emergency equipment should include a bumper or worm-type jack (make sure that all jack parts are in the vehicle, with the lug wrench next to it, tow rope or chain, and tire chains; and fire extinguisher. The tool kit should include all the wrenches and screwdrivers (especially Phillips) for every part of the vehicle, extra gas, and safety belts. Include extra fuses of the type used by your vehicle. The fuse box is usually under the dashboard, and major electrical failures often need but a replacement of a blown fuse. The first-aid supplies should be contained in a heavy metal box placed under the seat, behind the spare tire, or anyplace there is room, and passengers should be apprised of its location. The contents should include: assortment of bandages, gauze, adhesive tape, band-aids, absorbent pads, triangular bandage, burn ointment, and antiseptic lotion; also, a blanket to cover the ill or injured.

Should you be desert bound, water supply, obviously, should be figured amply over what you expect to use.

Once off the superhighway, remember that if you use a top carrier, periodically test the tie-down straps as well as all lashings and cover for the gear. Take it easy on boulder-strewn roads, and especially on crests of hills. On steep down-hill grades, don't ride the brakes; use lower gears.

The 4-WD vehicle permits the off-roader to range far in distance and in imagination in quest of his personal project. The versatile and dependable vehicle should not permit carelessness in planning that far-off adventure. A trail leader should be appointed, and he should make advance plans to cope with the unexpected. He, as the entire group, should know;

1. Who will take charge if the leader is injured?

2. Whom to notify first in case of accident or breakdown of vehicle?

3. Who will accompany an ill or injured party member (if able to travel) out of the woods or mountains?

4. What action to follow if the group becomes separated?

5. Who is responsible for hospital, doctor, and rescue bills?

*All races are not big-time; this one is a combined local race and family picnic.*

(Note: If airplanes are necessary, the cost will be $130 or more per hour. However, in some locales, military helicopters are available for life and death emergencies.)

The map of your proposed route should indicate the nearest ranger station, outfitter, farm or ranch, and road head, and the best route to get to these various places. Should a message for help be necessary, always write it out, and include your name and group, home address, age, and address of injured. Inform what happened, the condition and symptoms of the injured person(s), exactly what you have done, what is needed, and your exact location. Always send a party of at least two persons to deliver the message. *

## RACING

The racing aspect of 4-WD vehicles represents a highly specialized pursuit, and as in all vehicle discussion, will not be discussed beyond noting a few traditional races.

*Mexican 100*, from Tijuana to Ensenada, covers 67 miles of rugged terrain, and is usually held in November.

*Mint "400" Desert Rally* covers a 390-mile 1-lap course from Las Vegas to Beatty on the eastern edge of Death Valley. It is sponsored by the International Desert Racing Association of Nevada.

*National Off-Road Racing Association (NORRA)* race covers a 710-mile course similar to the Mint "400," but with a turn-around point to give the increased mileage.

*NORRA Mexican "1000"* race, on the Baja Peninsula, carries a total purse of approximately $60,000. It was recently covered by ABC's "Wide World of Sports" television program.

*NORRA Baja "500"* is roughly the first half of the Mexican "1000."

*Mint "400" Del Webb Desert Rally* covers 400 miles in 4 laps of 50 miles on each of 2 days. Total prize money of $50,000 is paid to the winners.

For further racing information contact: NORRA, 1616 Victory Blvd., Glendale, California, 91201.

## CLUBS AND ASSOCIATIONS

It is to the 4-WD vehicle owner's advantage to join a local club and regional and national associations. There you will meet members with a kindred vehicle and with similar recreation interests, and jointly will, no doubt, learn of the interesting ways in which you can participate: engage in service, fun, and off-road activities; establish trails and areas of participation; help in legislative matters; and improve the image of off-roading.

Clubs sponsor hillclimbs, slaloms, safaris, and gymkhanas on dunes and beaches, mountains and desert—and even on huge parking lots.

The format of the safari sponsored by the Tierra del Sol 4-WD Club of San Diego, California is typical. This annual desert safari through the Borrego Badlands of Southern California includes some 500 vehicles driving through a unique system of trail markers; green for the easier route and red for the more difficult trails (experts only). A 300-foot hill with talcum-powder-like surfaces and a 90° drop-off are included in the run. Straddling the ruts along the route is a required procedure to finish, which is usually around 8 hours after the starting gun goes off. Beginners and experts participate in the safari, and safety belts and roll bars have made it a safe one.

The Phoenix (Arizona) 4 Wheelers, a family-oriented group, sponsors an annual "4 Wheel Roundup" that is a week-long affair on the club's own land: 160 acres north of Wittman, Arizona, leased from the Bureau of Land Management. The rally is usually held before Easter of each year, and the interesting program includes low-key racing, rockhound hunts, a vehicle rodeo, and an Easter egg hunt for youngsters. In a recent rally the club hosted 1,200 people.

The improvement of leased land offers an excellent example of what an active club can do toward achieving acceptance by government agencies and local citizens while having a pleasant experience in the process. After acquiring the land in March, 1969, the P4W members set out with voluntary help and treasury funds to improve the site. Today, vehicle roads of varying nature crisscross the area, camping areas and restrooms are provided, and there is an enlarged outdoor dance floor for square dancing.

* Excerpted, in part, from "Leading a Back-country Outing," Forest Service, Intermountain Region, Department of Agriculture.

In Southern California, several 4-WD vehicle clubs recently met for a countryside cleanup and brought out a volume of trash that saved taxpayers an estimated $50,000. Many other clubs are concerned with environment and services. John Gaylord, commander of the Mile Hi Jeep Club in Boulder, Colorado, defending the 4-WD vehicle owners informs that, "Our particular group is more than just sensitive to conservation. We actively participate in road and trail repair, assist game and fish officials in natural habitat construction, restore historic structures, and sponsor a very large-scale trash and litter cleanup campaign. We have an annual conservation award, including a trophy and U.S. Savings Bond."

Most clubs under the Michigan 4-WD Association tend away from competition aspects, and stress more family outings. Clubs cruise the dune areas of Silver Lake and Lake Michigan, stop for a swim, then finish with a cook-out. Off-road weekend trips to the upper peninsula are popular, and when vehicles get stuck crossing a river or soft sand, other members are ready to winch out the mired vehicle. Club runs are popular in which messages are hidden in trees and bushes, giving instructions to the next point, as the caravan weaves up and down sand hills, through scrub forests, and along rivers, to finish with a picnic and activities for the children.

For further information contact:

National 4WD Assoc., Box 12798, Seattle, Washington, 98146.

Michigan 4WD Assoc., 936 Ireland Ave., Muskegon, Michigan, 49441.

National 4WD Assoc., Box 386, Rosemead, California, 91770.

THE 4-WD VEHICLE'S IMPACT ON ECOLOGY

That a vehicle weighing up to 5,000 pounds, with 4 driving and spinning tires can be very disruptive to natural terrain, is obvious. Misuse of 4-WD vehicles is a major problem in many parts of the United States where vast land areas are characterized by fragile ecosystems, loose soil, delicate plants, diminishing wildlife, and endangered birds.

That many 4-WD vehicle drivers have not used the land in a sportsman-like manner is indicated by the closure of much public land for their use. This reluctant decision on the part of officials occurred only after extreme damage was done.

Restrictions on vehicle use in 26 areas of Pike National Forest in Colorado were ordered in the summer of 1971. The acting forest supervisor of Colorado Springs was quick to add however, that, "The target of the limitations is the cross-country traveler who pits the machine against nature and desecrates the land in the process. For the most part, the restrictions apply to keeping the vehicles on the roads and trails. We're not prohibiting their use."

The district ranger at Leadville, Colorado announced the closing of 5 mountain areas to all mechanical vehicles. The closures, including a total of 25,100 acres, were made to protect the alpine tundra, prevent water erosion, and eliminate noise.

The regional forester of the Rocky Mountain region has specified 4-WD vehicle travel restrictions in 23.5 million acres of national forests in Colorado and Wyoming. He said, "We recognize these people and their right to use the national forests, but we also have an obligation to keep indiscriminate vehicle operators from tearing up the land, harassing game, and otherwise damaging resources that belong to everyone. The forests are simply being overrun by sheer numbers (of vehicles) in some areas, and a spider web of unmanageable roads is being developed as one motorized adventurer follows the trail of another."

These examples could be extended to include the Northeast, Southeast, Lake Central, Pacific Northwest, and Pacific Southwest regions of the national forests, though in varying degree.

The annual big game hunting seasons seem to bring out the worst in off-road travelers, especially with 4-WD vehicles. If no road exists where they want to go, they make one. Then the next driver, and many more after him, follow the ever-deepening trail. The Bureau of Land Management, Forest Service, and other public agencies report that the 4-WD vehicle is many times used as a bulldozer to push through pine and aspen stands; to gouge roads where the soil is wet from springs, seeps, or rainfall; and in general, to mar the good country—which is shrinking every day. Indiscriminate off-trail travel has resulted in limitations on vehicle use in increasing portions of public lands during various hunting seasons. This is particularly true of high-country, where reseeding efforts to reclaim ravaged land also result in closure to vehicles.

*On the Colorado Plateau, there is adequate 4-WD vehicle country, and recreation for every member of the family.*

It is often the single intruder, a gang, or an unaffiliated group, not an organized club, that does permanent damage to meadows, forest trails, stream banks, and terrain in general by improper use of vehicles. Today, much land is posted, definitely off-limits for any type of motorized vehicle. Some posted property carries a maximum penalty for trespassing of $500 and/or a 6-month jail sentence. The motorized recreation vehicle operator learns soon that many individuals and groups are in adamant opposition to motorized vehicles of any form.

As to litter problems, our booming packaging industries continue to bombard us with non-degradable packages and containers: aluminum, plastic, and glass throwaways. The 4-WD vehicle, as other motorized carriers, is capable of hauling into faraway places much of this eventual trash and leaving it there. True, there's little far-reaching destruction to litter, but the esthetic value alone is worth constant vigilance. Too, the attitude involved in "don't care about the next guy" in regard to litter will eventually pervade other, more vital, areas.

Motorized vehicles per se are accused of tearing up the soil; littering and fouling the quiet and pure air; endangering birds and animals; destroying wildlife habitat and plant life; causing erosion of land; and ruining the dignity, beauty, and serenity of wild places. All of this emphasizes again that man is by far the most crucial factor in the mechanized vehicle issue. He is solely responsible if the vehicle is used to violate the ecology of the land. Man is the manufacturer and user of vehicles, only he can control them.

As in most problems created by vehicles, the basic solution rests with the individuals involved, their personal sense of responsibility as embodied by the Golden Rule. Law enforcement officers confirm that the majority of vehicle drivers are conscientious about their housekeeping and abiding by the rules of the region. It is only a minuscule percentage of offenders that roar around clusters of population, litter trails and campsites, spook wildlife, and harass farm and ranch livestock. This minority of vehicle drivers, who hurt the image of off-roading, may not engage in delinquencies intentionally, but certainly thoughtlessly. The off-roader who observes the Golden Rule is doing his part to maintain the freedom of travel. "Use it, but don't abuse it . . . or you'll lose it" could well be the phrase for all mechanized off-road travelers.

## Some Positive Factors

The most encouraging aspect involving the misuse of 4-WD vehicles is the attention called to the problem.

The off-roader must guard zealously his privilege to use the millions of scenic acres. To illustrate the vast potential of off-road travel in national forest land, the closures in the Rocky Mountain region (indicated above) represent probably less than 10 percent of the land. Eleven million acres remain open for the prudent driver who stays on established roads and trails. Also in the national forests are many county, state, and federal roads, along with old mining roads, abandoned railroad grades, and lumbering roads, where the 4-WD vehicle is welcome. To keep it that way, the needs and rights of others must be recognized and respected. Otherwise, the wild freedom to roam, now enjoyed, may be drastically curtailed or completely eliminated. One forester believes, "We think for the most part the 4-WD groups are developing what I'd call an ethic."

The Colorado Open Roads Association (CORA) is one example of how 4-WD vehicle owners have organized to raise the image of off-roading, and extend experiences to children as well as adults. The estimated 130,000 adults and 77,000 children who ride 4-WD vehicles in pursuit of recreation should join an organization that stresses good manners on the trail, advocates self-policing in matters of environmental protection, and has consideration for the land.

You, as a 4-WD vehicle owner, spending as much time as possible in off-road areas, qualify as one of the wilderness cult, which knows that raw and untamed nature is a practical and useful resource that provides the body with exercise and the mind with peace.

## BUYER'S GUIDE

In considering the purchase of a 4-WD vehicle, there are so many options and accessories available that it is difficult to indicate a definite cost for the vehicle of your choice. A general rule is that the basic cost will be comparable to a conventional car, but extras will significantly raise the price.

As a prospective buyer of a 4-WD vehicle, you should realize that you'll be using the 4-WD approximately 1 mile for every 25 miles you drive a conventional 2-WD. The 4-WD option, which is expensive, is strictly for driving in difficult traction situations: mud, snow, sand, and steep grades. The decision to invest in the 4-WD option should be determined by the amount of use it will be given.

**Jeep** (American Motors Corp., 14250 Plymouth Road, Detroit, Michigan, 48232) models include the Commando which comes in 3 body styles (station wagon, pickup, and roadster), and the CJ-5 and CJ-6. All are designed for the rapidly rising recreational vehicle market.

Since the acquisition of Jeep by American Motors, the 4-WD vehicles have undergone many changes and refinements: to accommodate the new American Motors engines, and to improve riding quality, the wheelbase, overall length, and tire tread of models have been increased. All engines meet or exceed requirements of Federal exhaust emission controls. Power steering and power brakes are offered.

In the line-up of recreational off-road models, there is a choice of 3 engines. The 6-cylinder is standard, while another 6 (258 CID) and 8-cylinder are optional. Standard transmission is a floor-mounted 3-speed manual, full synchromesh. A floor-mounted 4-speed manual transmission is optional with both 6-cylinder engines.

Recently innovated improvements include: new flanged-shaft rear axle with capacity increased to 3,000 pounds; new increased capacity 10.5" clutch for all engines; new increased capacity 11" service brakes for improved braking performance and service life; suspended clutch and brake pedal controls; and improved heater.

New options include: solid, fixed tailgate with rear tailgate-mounted spare wheel and tire; more durable Whitco vinyl-coated, fabric full top; 15" wheel covers; cigarette lighter and ashtray; oil and ammeter gauges.

Base price: pickup, $3,900; station wagon, $4,200.

**Blazer** (Chevrolet Motor Div., G.M.C., General Motors Bldg., Detroit, Michigan 48202) is a newcomer in the 4-WD vehicle field, and breaks away

BELOW: *Jeep*
RIGHT: *Blazer*

from many typical "jeep" characteristics, being based instead on pickup truck chassis, body lines, and construction. Advantages include stability, a wider wheelbase, and more room behind the front seats (over 6 feet of open bed length at floor level, which is large enough to accommodate a full-length mattress for the off-roader who wants to set up shelter and housekeeping in the boondocks).

Standard equipment includes a 6-cylinder engine (2 optional V-8 engines are available). Transmission is 3-speed manual with a steering column-mounted shift lever. Such truck components as heavy-gauge steel frame, tapered leaf springs, double wall construction, and built-in fender liners that resist rust and wear, make the Blazer an ideal package as well as a trailer-hauling vehicle.

Both front and rear brakes are self-adjusting. The rear brakes are finned for better cooling, and there is improved recovery from the effects of water, salt, and slush because of the spinning action of the rotating brake disc. A 3-way fluid valve balances the entire braking system, proportions front and rear braking pressures, and warns of pressure loss in either half of the system.

Accessories to make a complete vehicle include power steering, free-wheeling front hubs, fiberglass hardtop, canvas soft top, heavy-duty springs and shock absorbers, auxiliary battery, passenger bucket seats, radio, passenger arm rest, front towing hooks, and wide wheels and tires.

Options for the extra demands of off-road driving

and camping include heavy-duty 12-volt battery, shock absorbers, clutch, generator, air cleaner, and air conditioning.

Base price: 6-cyl., 2-WD, $2,726; 6-cyl., 4-WD, $3,301; 8-cyl., 2-WD, $2,847; 8-cyl., 4-WD, $3,422.

**Bronco** (Ford Division, Rotunda Drive at Southfield, Dearborn, Michigan, 48121) has all the features of your passenger car: pushbutton door locks, top-pivoted wipers, pedal-operated parking brake, column shift, and gauges. And for comfort and safety, there is a day/night rearview mirror, padded shelf on top of the instrument panel, arm rests, roll-down windows, and no-draft vents, along with coil springs on the front axle.

The Bronco comes in 2 body styles (open pickup and hardtop wagon) with an 8 hp engine option. 4-WD is standard. Featured are an all-welded frame in one complete box section throughout its length, sturdy roof, eight rubber-cushioning body mounts, and a positive locking device that helps prevent accidental jumping out of 4-WD gear.

Bronco's heavy-duty front axle and suspension provide strength to withstand severe off-road punishment such as steep climbing and sudden descents on difficult roads. The short wheelbase (92"), adequate ground clearance, underside protection, and wide-set tires permit the vehicle to maneuver on slopes, negotiate difficult trails, and climb over peaked projections without hanging up amidships.

For extensive off-road use, the Bronco can be

ABOVE: *Bronco*
RIGHT: *Land Rover*

equipped with heavy-duty rear axle and springs, and large 8.25 x 15-D 8-ply tires with mud or snow patterns.

For extensive city and family use, a sport package should be considered; it includes vinyl door trim panels with bright metal moldings, parchment vinyl front floor mat, chrome bumpers, painted grille, cigarette lighter, and various lighting features.

Dealer-installed accessories include overload air-bags for the front suspension, front power-take-off and winch, 2-way radio, compass and tachometer, exterior-mounted swing-away spare tire carrier, trailer hitch, and snowplow.

Base price: pickup model, $3,150; hardtop model, $3,200.

**Land Rover** (British Leyland Motors Inc., 600 Willow Tree Road, Leonia, New Jersey, 07605), in its deluxe version, features a hardtop model that seats 7, and, for off-road adventuring, can carry a payload of 3 persons and 800 pounds of equipment.

Power is supplied from a 4-cylinder engine with overhead inlet and exhaust valves. Transmission to front and rear axles is by open propeller shaft via 2-speed transfer box, and there are 4 forward speeds and reverse. A 2-speed transfer box in conjunction with the main gearbox gives 8 forward speeds and 2 reverse.

Many standard features are included: security catches and door locks; side-hinged rear door with

external locking handle; two forward adjusting front seats; two folding, side-facing, rear bench seats; rubber carpet (front and rear), shoulder and lap safety harnesses for two front seats; hazard warning and dual braking system; backup lights; windshield washers; oil pressure gauge; tool kit; jack and emergency starting crank; towing pintle; heater and defroster, Goodyear 7.10" x 15" tires, and some other items.

Optional (factory fitted) extra equipment includes heavy-duty rear springs, front and rear shock absorbers, rear power take-off (for attachment of power tools), tropical roof, folding steps for side doors, 8-bladed fan, radio interference suppressors, rear step, twin horns, locking hasp for fuel filler, flyscreens for dash vents, and many others.

These items, when fitted during vehicle production, are much cheaper than when locally installed since shipment of parts plus labor costs are expensive.

Base price: $4,100.

**Land Cruiser** (Toyota Motor Sales, U.S.A. Inc., 2055 West 190th St., Torrence, California, 90501) boasts of a ride that is reasonably free of pitch and harshness, and its power-operated transfer-case controls, conveniently placed below the instrument panel, with a warning light for 4-WD, offer a boon to the off-roader.

Known as the best buy (pricewise) of any 4-WD vehicle, the Land Cruiser is characterized by truck design features: firm boxy body, rugged metal interior, and absence of trim and upholstery. A 6 cyl. engine drives the vehicle at an 80 mph cruising speed. You have 6 forward gears and 2 reverse, and when steep road conditions require 4-WD, you simply pull the convenient "FD" knob to negotiate grades up to 71°.

The hardtop and soft top models have a 90" wheelbase which gives little passenger and cargo space behind the front seats, and carries the hardride characteristics of the original jeep and all contemporary short wheelbase vehicles. The Land Cruiser Station Wagon model, with its 104" wheelbase, is ideal for the off-road explorer who wishes a dependable ride and a vehicle he can live in.

A limited number of factory-installed options are available: power take-off and winch, heater, and mud or snow tires. Independent accessory shops can fill you in with luggage racks, gas can holders, radio, roll bars, etc.

Base price: soft top, $3,300; hardtop, $3,500; wagon, $4,300.

**Scout** (International Harvester Co., Chicago, Illinois, 60611) has been on the outdoor scene for over 20 years, and comes from a family of many farm machines and heavy-duty trucks. The Scout comes in hardtop, open roadster, and pickup models and is powered by a 4-cylinder engine that is intended for low-speed off-highway use. The standard transmission is 3-speed manual, but there are two options: a 4-speed manual and a 3-speed automatic. The wheelbase measures 100", and ground clearance is 7.1".

The Scout best serves the rural customer since it includes many features for outdoor work as standard. Among these are front and rear power take-offs for a post hole auger, mower, sweeper, or snowplow. On the underside of the vehicle, a reinforced welded plate protects the vital mechanisms of transmission, transfer case, and crankcase from rocks, logs, and high-crowned roads. The radiator is protected in front and underneath by a steel cross-member and heavy steel flange.

For extensive off-road use, the following options should be considered: heavy-duty battery, alternator, front and rear springs, super-wide tires, and a second gas tank.

International also offers a superhighway-suburban-status model, Aristocrat, which is available with a large horsepower engine. The Aristocrat includes a

*Dodge W-200*

Powr-Lok limited-slip differential, chrome bumpers, carpeting, dual 10-gallon gas tanks, free-wheeling front hubs, luggage rack, radio, rear seat, outside tire carrier, chrome wheels, undercoating, and 5 wide oval custom tires.

Base price: 2-WD, $2,800; 4-WD, $3,500.

**Dodge W-200** (Dodge Div. Chrysler Corp., Box 1259, Detroit, Michigan, 48231) is built more like a commercial pickup truck than a typical off-road vehicle. Models range from 114" to 165" in wheelbase, and can be bought with bare chassis and cab to offer a wide berth in attaching a variety of camper rigs and shell shelters. In that way, a sturdy 4-WD camper, tailor-made, is achieved.

The standard engine is 6-cylinder, and 2 8-cylinder engines are offered as options. Transmission is a 3-speed manual, with options of a 4-speed manual and a 3-speed automatic.

The Camper Special model is offered for off-road use. It includes limited-slip differential, heavy-duty battery and alternator, power brake booster, tachometer, oil pressure gauge, power take-off, and heavy-duty springs.

A Custom Interior Package is available and it includes rubber floor mats, bright molding, additional insulation, air conditioning, seat cushions, and tinted windshield.

Base price: 2-WD, $3,200; 4-WD, $3,500.

*Optional Equipment and Accessory Sources*

The manufacturer of your vehicle is probably the best source for accessories, options, and decorative items. However, sometimes items can be bought more economically from other sources, which also may include a greater diversity of products:

Sears, Roebuck and Co., Dept. 139, 925 S. Homan Ave., Chicago, Illinois, 60607

Warshawsky & Co., 1900 S. State St., Chicago, Illinois, 60616

Motion Minicar Corp., 594 Sunrise Highway, Baldwin, New York, 11510

# 6. THE DUNE BUGGY

The dune buggy received its greatest notoriety when astronauts David R. Scott and James B. Irwin left Apollo 15 on July 31, 1971 to explore the moon's surface in a 9-million-dollar moon buggy.

The moonwalk became a buggy ride as the astronauts bounced their moon vehicle at 7 mph to the brink of a canyon and the dusty base of a moon mountain. In two days of riding and walking the lunar surface and picking up rock samples, the ultimate in dune buggying (and in rockhounding) was reached. ". . . it's a sporty job to drive," said Scott, after covering 5 miles of lunar surface the first day.

Extensive explorations were possible with the battery-driven buggy, which performed well in the tricky and powdery terrain of the moon. In touring to Hadle Rille, 1 mile across and 1,200 feet deep, many previously unknown geological features were observed, and rock samples were garnered—all through the advantage of a highly specialized dune buggy.

Back to the planet Earth, we find that the dune buggy came into large-scale popularity in 1966 to provide sand-scooting fun for young men and women, parents, and youngsters. Their area of operation was the hills, deserts, mountains, beaches, and sand dunes in various parts of the country. Where dunes are unknown, the vehicle is called a "sand buggy." Today, several hundred thousand are registered, giving rise to the term, "buggy generation."

Buggying began on the sands of Pismo Beach, California and Yuma, Arizona before World War II. Garage mechanics used a conventional car, shortened the frame, and added huge tires. After that, war surplus jeeps were used, to be followed in the early 1950s by the cut-down frame and stripped-down Volkswagen. Many innovations in body design gave the mechanic a tailor-made buggy for off-road riding, but if he desired to make the buggy legal for street use, it was necessary to add bumpers, headlights, turn signals, horn, windshield and wipers, muffler, and emergency brake.

In recent years, dune buggies have come a long way: from ugly cold frames and angular sheet metal bodies to sporty cars with original and interesting designs; from purely dune riders to rakish highway-riding sports cars. It is estimated that only 20 percent of the buggies are used in off-road pursuits, including racing, and 80 percent are used for street and highway travel.

Dune buggies that are road licensable can be driven to the area of participation. Those that are made strictly for off-road use, less ornate and cheaper in price, must be trailered or towed on the highway.

## CHARACTERISTICS OF A DUNE BUGGY

The development of the dune buggy was influenced by the need of man to climb sand dunes and cross otherwise impassable deserts and hills. This function determined its many unique characteristics: light weight; short wheelbase; engine, transmission, and differential in the rear over the driving wheels; and no weight on the front wheels, which are used only for steering.

To qualify as a dune buggy a vehicle must meet certain power and design specifics including rear engine drive. The Volkswagen is mostly used, but Corvette, Porsche, V-4 Ford, Simca, and Opel engines, which are more expensive, are also used. A chassis from the Volkswagen is generally cut in half, the middle section cut off, then welded back together for a shortened chassis. The original sheet metal body is replaced by a fiberglass shell of varied styles; some are topless and most of these have a roll bar, others are roofed, and still others are austere by their lack of any superstructure.

Large rear tires best characterize a dune buggy; they offer suitable traction, high ground clearance, and permit a large "footprint" which does little to disrupt the driving surface. The majority of tires conform to one of three basic designs (bias, bias-belted, or radial) referring to the manner in which the rayon, nylon, fiberglass, or steel cords are laid in the carcass. The bias tire is most commonly used, and the least expensive. As to price, tires range from $25 (apiece) for the conventional 8.25" x 15" size to $125 per tire for the huge 31" x 15" size. There are a hundred sizes in between.

If you are using the dune buggy for a lot of off-road driving, the surface can vary from muck to gravel, sand to silt, with jagged rocks and steep grades. Therefore, the rear tires, where the weight is concentrated and the power reaches the ground, must be super-wide, high-flotation, almost like balloons. The front tires need not be as large.

Tires should be tubeless and filled with puncture sealant, but if a puncture occurs, stick in a boot, then a tube. Off-road, when far from a filling station, a tire can be inflated by screwing an air hose into a spark plug hole for induction of air by piston action.

The buggy that is used in off-trail places must be equipped with roll bars, safety belts, and an adequate engine. The driver and passengers must wear crash helmets, long-sleeved shirts, sturdy trousers, and ankle-top shoes.

## A TINKERER'S DREAM

Mechanical-minded devotees of the dune buggy have taken the vehicle, in design and use, far beyond the "take the family on a Sunday spin" phase. The do-it-yourself young men have parlayed their "know how" as well as their whims to create conservative, utilitarian, or "way out" designs featuring souped-up engines, heavy springs, slick-looking body shells, over-size tires, and decor from bumper to bumper. The ardent buggy builder is constantly on the lookout for engines, transmissions, and chassis components that offer a "first" possibility for his creation. Accessories are his "bag" and they include a wide array of functional and decorative additions: convertible tops, huge tires, bucket seats, stabilizers, covers, and on and on the list goes.

These young men, by and large, find their way to the many highly-touted races and become quasi-professional competitors, who drive across the country from California to Florida with stops in between. They compete locally too, in slalom, drag, enduro, and cross-country races for trophies, merchandise, and cash.

## DUNE BUGGY KITS

The kit to build a dune buggy can cost anywhere from a couple hundred dollars to a couple of thousand. Complete instructions about shortening the Volkswagen or conventional car body frame and assembling the buggy atop it are included. There are over fifty buggy bodies (mostly fiberglass shells) on the market. Since few dealers sell complete cars, the dune buggy game is largely a build-it-yourself project—in a barn, garage, or backyard. Your buggy's appearance will be determined by the options with the kit. Some prospective buggy owners buy additional options to completely enclose the cab, and install a heater for year-round use. Kits include various styles and shapes of body in two dozen different colors, flake paint, mag wheels, racing steering wheels, psychedelic tops, and chromed exhausts. Most companies promise in their kits modern styling, quality components, 100-percent resin and fiberglass bodies, high-quality hoods and fenders, high-impact dashboards, windshields, wide tires, roll bar, and a choice of colors. The following instructions were provided by Sand Pounders, Inc. of Wheeling, Illinois.

Kits are offered in "A" and "B" stages. The "A" kit for approximately $300 includes the basic body, hood, and dashboard. The "B" kit for approximately $380 more completes the buggy, and includes windshield frame, headlights, fliptop gas cap, nuts, bolts, screws, fender welting, roll bar, bumpers, convertible top, seats, and lights.

The electrical system represents the heart of the vehicle. Follow judiciously the instructions, as there are many variations in the wire looms of various kits. The most expensive dune buggy will not perform efficiently if the electrical system is improperly installed.

Most dune buggy builders use the conventional VW engine, but for the speed fan, hopping up the buggy has been going on for over 20 years. In order to get more power than the VW engine delivers, some souping-up projects are necessary: improved air intakes, larger bore of

*The Four-Corners Area offers a buggy land with colorful rock formations and solid trails.*

# CONSTRUCTION OF A DUNE BUGGY

First step in building your buggy is to install the gas tank. A 1961 or newer is needed. A 1962 or newer will give you a gas gauge. Filler neck may be left in original position, or use a new flip top cap in a new position. If a new charger is to be used, cut off the original filler neck flush with the tank. Place gas tank in body. Set hood in place. Drill a 2" hole where gas cap is to be installed. Place 1⅞" tubing (supplied by us with purchase of kit) in hole so it is resting on tank. Use a can of spray paint, and spray down into the tubing. This will mark the proper position for the new filler. Now weld original filler neck hole shut. Weld new filler in place. (If no welding facilities are available, bring it to us. Cost—$10.00.) Install gas tank in body. Bolt securely in place using rectangular body washers from original VW.

You are now ready to put hood in place. Drill 7 holes on each side of the body along the line, and ¼" below where the hood meets the body as indicated by arrow in Diagram #1. Use a ⁵⁄₁₆" size drill bit. Set hood in place. Be sure it fits tightly. If hood does not fit tightly in place due to hitting gas tank, remove hood and *reshape front corners of the tank with a large hammer*. With the hood in position, very carefully work fender welting into place on one side (using screwdrivers to separate hood and body enough to get welting in place). Use ⅛" drill bit to drill holes for hood attachment. This is done by drilling through the ⁵⁄₁₆" holes, but from the underside

of the body. Use screws supplied with kit as each hole is drilled. Do same on the other side. Hood is now permanently in place.

Next item install headlights, turn signals, tail lights, license plate lights, speedometer and gauges, and any other electrical components you plan on using. (Best method for installing speedometer is two lumps of body filler on the back side over the ears on speedometer case to the dash.)

Now turn body upside down on saw horses using wire loom. *Do not use old VW wires*. Loom supplied by us contains complete instructions for wiring. *ALL WIRING SHOULD BE SOLDERED*.

With the wiring completed, turn body right side up and place on chassis. Bolt down with bolts supplied in kit using ⁵⁄₁₆". To locate proper hole alignment, drill from bottom side of the floor pan through original VW holes.

With body in place, your next step is to install steering column. If hole is cut in dash VERY CAREFULLY, steering column will fit securely and not require any dash brace. Drill ¼" hole in fire wall for steering column. Use a stiff piece of wire through dash and fire wall to steering box. Move hole in fire wall as needed to make a straight line between center of hole in dash and center of steering box.

Next step install windshield at same angle as hood dash seam. Use ⁵⁄₁₆" bolts and large washers on the inside. See Diagram #2 for exact measurements.

# CONSTRUCTION OF A DUNE BUGGY

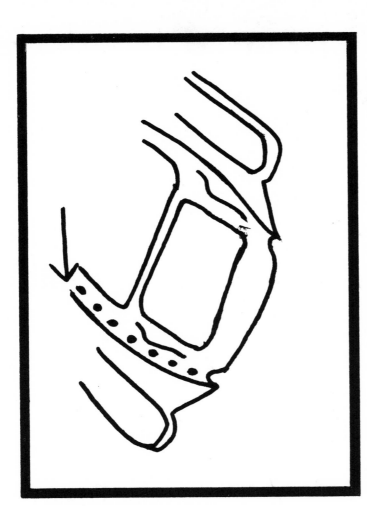

**DIAGRAM #1**

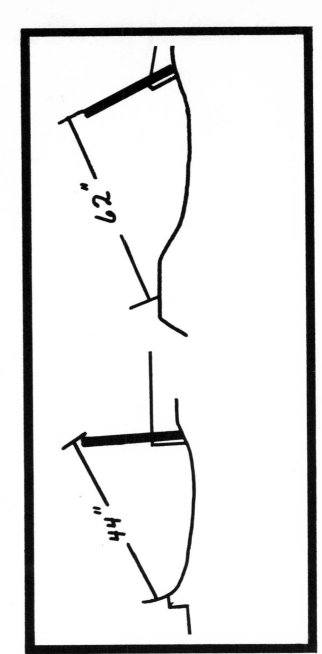

**DIAGRAM #2**

*Baja country, south of the border, is known for its excellent beaches.*

cylinders and pistons, hot cams, larger carburetor and manifold, a longer stroke crankshaft, and extractor exhaust represent the major alterations.

Two weekends with the aid of a son or neighbor are generally required to complete the job. Building your buggy calls for much involvement with assembly, wiring, bolting down the engine of your choice, building the body from a crate of fiberglass panels, welding, bolting, and gluing. The construction stages, along with the sharing of ideas with many persons, add up to a lot of personal satisfaction—rarely experienced by the man who buys a complete vehicle.

As a prospective buyer of a dune buggy kit, patronize your local (or nearest) dealer, rather than shopping for a better price in some distant geographical locale. The cost of building a shipping crate for the 125 to 150-pound body in the approximate dimensions of 11' x 5' x 2½', and paying the freight charges, will offset the price of the most appealing distant source offered. In recent years, freight lines have increased their charges for delivering a dune buggy kit by approximately 400 percent.

Accessories for the dune buggy are without comparison in extent or imagination. They include such items as a support frame for windshield and hood and dash, convertible top with side curtains, roll bar, car cover, heavy-duty springs, stabilizers, shock absorbers, hub caps, wheel covers, wide dish wheels, slotted wheels, hot cams, extra-wide custom wheels, wide-track tires, close ratio gears, dual exhausts, air cleaner, bucket seats, nylon carpets, various gauges, tow bar, storage side pockets, spark arrester exhaust, skid plate, wiring harness, power brakes, headlamps, lift or lowering kit, etc.

## AREAS OF PARTICIPATION

Dune buggy owners, especially in crowded metropolitan areas, have the problem of finding a suitable stretch of sand for their activities. The vehicle isn't welcome on the average beach, horseback or hiking trail, or many other places. This problem may impose a limitation or ceiling on dune buggy popularity and ownership, but the industry expects a 300,000 market by 1975.

Government and state land agencies are aware of the growing interest in outdoor recreation and realize that much of the remaining open space is in itself a resource that could possibly be used with proper husbandry by the off-road enthusiast. A few possibilities for adventurous buggying follow.

*The deserts* of the Southwest represent the buggy owner's sea, a shifting expanse, rippled and moving, that has a sense of infinity all its own. For one, the Desert Foothills Drive out of Scottsdale, Arizona is claimed by residents to be one of the most beautiful on the continent, abounding in mesquite, gray thorn, jumping cholla, and giant saguaro cactus.

*The Slick Rock Trail* in the Moab, Utah region also represents a buggy land with regional uniqueness: colorful rock formations, solid trails, ample campsites, and hospitable natives (see also Chapter 9).

*The Four-Corners Area* (Colorado, Utah, Arizona, and New Mexico) represents the land of the Navajos which has uranium riches, colorful canyons, wild rivers, a surviving narrow-gauge railroad, many national monuments, the Million Dollar Highway, and shadows of once-rich mining towns.

Interstate Highway 70 takes you to the edge of this realm, and from there the dune buggy leads through awe-inspiring high country—the greatest concentration of scenic wonders in the world. For further information contact: The Golden Circle Assoc., Box 111, Moab, Utah, 84532.

*The Big Sur* country in California, from San Luis Obispo to the Monterey Peninsula on U.S. Highway 101, is famous for its scenery and is lavished with the ever-recurring Pacific Ocean surf. The route is redolent with cool forests of redwood and pine, crags pointing to the sky, stunted cypress hanging on the bluffs, and frothy seascapes below. For 129 spectacular miles, the road curves along ocean coves, through narrow scrub brush canyons, and high overlooks where you can gaze at the surf in solitude. It's not a road for hurrying.

Along the narrow road, parking spaces and oceanside campgrounds are ample (on week-days), and sea otters are often visible from shore. This, too, is the land of the condor, and perhaps you can see this disappearing and endangered species.

The Big Sur is visited by many, but it remains unspoiled by population hordes. Man does not change scenery like this; it looks much the same as it did when the Spaniards first came up the same coastline some 300 years ago.

*Baja country*, also called Baja Peninsula or Lower California, is extolled in dune buggy lore, for this area too has changed little over the centuries. The finger of harsh but exotic land stretches for 800 miles south from the California border. Its width varies from about 200 to 400 miles and it is bounded on the west by the Pacific Ocean and on the east by the Gulf of California, a prolific deep-sea fishing water. A spur of mountains slopes toward the ocean, and both coastlines have hundreds of coves, bays, and excellent beaches.

Each year thousands of dune buggy enthusiasts make the Baja trip to experience the contrast of arid desert and lush green areas and to savor the particular intimacy of the land with the sea.

Beyond the populated northern portion of Baja, south of El Rosario, you may travel for days without seeing another person. Obviously, the tour becomes a wilderness project and is recommended for experienced off-road drivers with a dependable vehicle and adequate provisions—especially water and purifying Halzone tablets. However, the sights you see will be those viewed by few stateside citizens.

With proper planning, the Baja sojourn can be the most rewarding experience you ever had. As the trip is beyond our border, no difficulty should be encountered if a few details of planning are followed. Get the latest data (which changes frequently) from the Mexican Consul or at the U.S. border stations at the point of entry.

Such matters as touring cards, insurance, and car permits are vital considerations, most of which can be resolved at the border inspection stations for both countries located at Tijuana, Tecate, Algodones, and Mexicali. The offices are open 7 days a week: Tijuana and Mexicali around the clock, Algodones 8 A.M. to 6 P.M., Tecate 8 A.M. to midnight. Don't attempt to cross the border on Sunday if your time is limited: delays of several hours are common. Further in-

*Cruising the clean stretches of sand near Mazatlan*

formation on import regulations, photography, duty-free merchandise, fishing permits, firearms, inoculations, etc. can be obtained from the Mexican Government Tourism Dept, Box 75552, Stanton Station, Los Angeles, California, 90005.

*Mazatlan, Mexico*, on the west coast of the mainland, directly across from the tip of Baja, and approximately 800 miles south of the border is another exceptional land that has been "discovered" by dune buggy adventurers.

Most use Mazatlan as their base. From here they roam the unspoiled rural areas, where the sight of a dune buggy brings out crowds of curious Mexicans of all ages. Highway pavement is in short stretches, so you use the dirt roads, untended and ungraded, with the agile dune buggy to cruise across clean stretches of beach, past harbors for deep-sea fishing fleets, up the rocky hills for sweeping views of sea and landscape, then to the backcountry villages.

Hire a local guide, particularly for the mountain trails in the Durango area that lead off the main highway to heavily wooded land, past streams and waterfalls, mining camps, ancient churches, and quaint villages deep in lush jungle canyons. Ever-present are the raucous colorful birds, a profusion of wild flowers, and myriads of tropical palms.

Activities for a change of pace include: waterskiing, fishing, swimming, skindiving, and at day's end, dining and dancing on a terrace overlooking the sea.

Beyond these experiences, there is the Mazatlan, or rather the Mexican, philosophy of disdain for the calendar, clock, hurry, and fret that will haunt you on the homeward trek as you plan for the next trip.

Similar experience possibilities with your dune buggy exist along the shores of the Great Lakes; the grass, sand, and swamplands of Florida; the beaches along the Atlantic coast; and even in the prairie states of the Midwest. They lie within a day's drive from urban areas and include secluded byways, scenic drives, and interesting places to visit or picnic, or just to commune with nature. Close to home, all that is required is for your dune buggy club to search out a unique piece of land, obtain permission for its use, set up self-policing rules, and fill up the gas tank.

## CLUBS

California alone has some 80 or more organized local clubs, many comprised of family-member couples. Clubs, in general, follow an interesting schedule of activities of fun and service: safety and vehicle inspections, picnics and barbecues, youth driving clinics, treasure hunts, conservation outings, parade participation, litter clean-up, and intra-club rallies.

These are only a few of the activities organized, conducted, and supervised by the various officers of the particular group. In addition to "fun" activities, many clubs are conscientious in their efforts to serve: to work on trails, charitable drives, conservation programs, and in the area of search and rescue, to cooperate with local law enforcement agencies by offering their buggies for travel in areas inaccessible to cars and trucks.

Many clubs on their scheduled trips are dedicated to hauling out more litter than they bring in, and one club (Nor-Cal Nomads) organized a group of 500 people in an estimated 300 vehicles and removed 10 large truckloads of litter from the Marina Beach Sand Dunes, a popular area for off-road activity.

Another three-day work-play event was organized by the California Off-Road Vehicle Association and drew more than 725 registered participants from 21 dune buggy clubs and 1 Explorer Scout Troop. The volunteers picked up 17 1-ton truckloads and 6 pickup loads of trash and litter, estimated at 150 cubic yards. Large 3-ply paper bags, used for broken glass and irregularly shaped junk were furnished by a local chemical company. The volunteers donated an estimated 2,900 man hours for the cleanup, and the value of the labor was conservatively estimated at $6,000.

Your best approach to club participation is to query your local association (see Appendix) or ask a local dealer for the name and address of the nearest organized group.

The club aspect of dune buggying will become more popular in the coming years, according to the California Off-Road Vehicle Association. "Because this sport is so attractive to families, it may very well be that . . . 80 percent of the population within the state will either own, build, or use some type of off-road vehicle." They further add, "Within this busy, rapid-pace, hectic society of the 20th century today, the society of the 'ulcer and the migraine,' not to mention the 'hippie and the juvenile delinquent,' every family needs a diversion, a change of scene—the off-roaders feel they have found it."

## THE DUNE BUGGY'S IMPACT ON ECOLOGY

Due to the pressure of off-road activity in many areas, especially upon state and federal lands, it has become necessary to enforce more diligently laws already on the books, as well as many new regulations, for the ecological protection of the lands. There are many off-road vehicles that are more numerous, and inherently more destructive, than the dune buggy, yet it has the longest history of local-use restrictions.

"The Off-road Vehicle and Environmental Quality," a report published by The Conservation Foundation, 1717 Massachusetts Ave. N.W., Washington, D.C., 20036, deals with the social and environmental effects of off-road vehicles, and states, ". . . ecological realities must be faced in man's need and search for places to refresh his life, sense his identity with other life and the earth, and to understand his historical and cultural links with past and future men. These places must be free from the shattering influence of incompatible machines."

The Foundation further claims, "The phenomenon of the off-road vehicle reflects a misplaced sense of national priorities, responding neither to this country's problems of decay and social dismay, nor to the world's need for its own help in arresting its pollution and human misery."

The off-road automotive problem involves more than 3 million motorized recreational vehicles, which are causing a host of serious environmental problems, some new and others old, but nearly all, difficult to solve.

The apprehensions of The Conservation Foundation are echoed by many others, national and local agencies, by environment groups and individuals, and by observers and scholars.

Larry E. Moss, Southern Representative, Sierra Club, believes that, "Vehicle users should ask for restriction and reasonable zoning of uses or they face expulsion from the public lands. . . . A system of zoning that maximizes protection of natural and historical values must be instituted on all public lands. They are held in trust by the nation, and it is not for this or any generation to

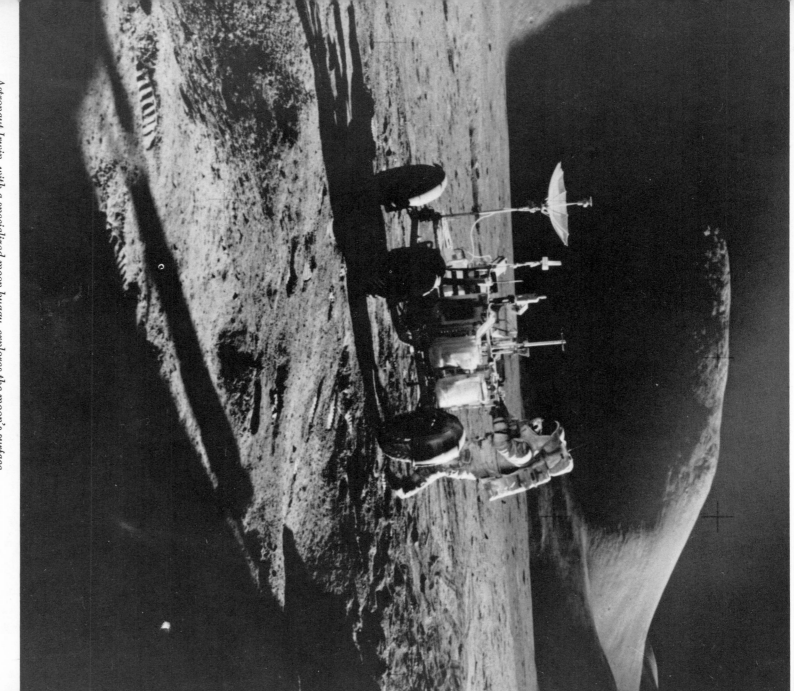

Astronaut Irwin, with a specialized moon buggy, explores the moon's surface.
NASA PHOTO

thoughtlessly destroy them. All user groups must, to a great degree, police themselves and actively protect the resources which support their use."

Many coastal and lake states complain that dune buggies tear up vegetation and beach grasses, creating blowouts and erosion. They level dunes and disturb the natural contours of the region, and they are noisy, destructive, and dangerous.

States with arid terrains claim that fragile vegetation has been denuded from desert areas by unthoughtful and irresponsible buggy drivers —vegetation that will recover very, very slowly under these ravaging onslaughts.

The Forest Service states that the wear and erosion of a trail by one improperly used vehicle is equivalent to that of 10 or 15 hikers.

The Bureau of Sport Fisheries and Wildlife (Southeastern Division) has "the responsibility of closing any refuge area that is open to off-road vehicle use if such becomes necessary or desirable for the prevention of erosion, the protection of other resources, or the furtherance of other Bureau activities."

The Bureau's Conservation Education Coordinator, Donald W. Pfitzer, informs, "We have had some real problems at Back Bay Wildlife Refuge (Virginia Beach) where the use of dune buggies has caused serious trouble on the sand dunes."

The elk hunting season in the Steamboat Mountain area of Wyoming was canceled when the state game and fish commission discovered that "Dune buggies have driven practically all of the elk herd out of the region." From a herd of between 350 and 400 elk, only 35 remained in the area.

Many seashore communities have enacted stringent laws affecting dune buggy activity. The Massachusetts Beach Buggy Association, one of the first on the East Coast and with a membership of around 2,000, has been declining because of the increasing restrictions for their use.

Closure of the Bruneau Dunes State Park in southwestern Utah to all off-road vehicles was announced in 1971.

In California, it has become necessary for the Bureau of Land Management, State Park System, and Recreation Commission to rigidly enforce existing regulations in certain areas of misuse, and to set forth new restrictions in others. And legislation control is indicated by the House of

Representatives Bill #9661, Assembly Bills #2342 and #2787, and Senate Bill #504.

It is interesting to note that among dune buggy owners, there are many who use it as a family-fun vehicle, and they seem to be sensitive to proper participation. Evidently it is a small percentage of hot-rodders that contribute to environment-destroying shenanigans, and a lowered image.

The science of ecology notes that the earth is constantly changing; lakes become euthropic, rivers become clogged with silt, mountains erode, and forests age. Offsetting this is the constant rate of natural rejuvenation which ideally insures a balance of birth and death. However, population pressures and over-use and misuse by mechanical vehicles of certain areas highly accelerate the problems of ecology.

Ecosystems vary from locale to locale. Areas where the growing season is long, the rainfall adequate, and brush cover and established grasses are suitable recover sooner than those in high altitudes, arid or semi-arid areas, certain seashores, or salt marshes. Participation on these fragile lands, therefore, implies responsible and non-destructive use.

Some critics of off-road vehicles claim that wear and tear on land is irreparable. They say it as if opinion is fact. But consider a few examples: Panoche Hills, in central California foothill country, has served vehicle traffic for over a decade, with as many as 2,000 vehicles in a month. Closure for reseeding the hills is practiced and makes the area reusable over and over again.

The southwestern deserts, in close proximity to large population centers, receive intensive use for dune buggy cross-country racing, hill climbs, enduros, etc. When sites were carefully chosen, destruction to the terrain was negligible. An example is found in Pomo Dunes near Pismo Beach, California, which has been popular with vehicle operators for many years and has few problems.

Lieutenant General F. J. Clarke, Chief of Engineers, Dept. of Army, at Corvallis, Oregon in speaking to the Universities Council on Water Resources on the water permit program and total environment impacts, indicated that no one person, organized group, or governmental agency can take on the whole job of marshaling society's endeavors to improve the environment. An equal share remains for each of them. It is basically the individual who must supply the knowledge and the truths which governmental agencies can apply. Many people are going too fast, demanding action to help the environment today, and growing numbers of them are becoming dissatisfied with the lack of visible results. One main key to better results is more knowledge, obtainable only through more sound research.

Clarke concluded, "Your government's environment programs all admittedly have a considerable element of experiment in them at this stage. We want to improve and refine them. If you wish to sit back and criticize, you will find plenty of ground for doing so. Indeed, you may well find the government itself way ahead of you in criticism, in spotting flaws, and pointing them out. But we know you will want to do something more. We hope you will want to join us in a cooperative endeavor in which each acts in co-operation, toward the achievement of practical, pragmatic results that will be beneficial to and acceptable by the people as a whole."

## BUYER'S GUIDE

Many companies offer dune buggy kits and accessories. A few regional sources are here listed.

### Far West
Bandito, 8847 9th St., Cucamonga, California, 91730
Barris Buggies, 2060 Westwood Blvd., Los Angeles, California, 90025
Boondocker, 186 E. Sunnyoaks Ave., Campbell, California, 95008
Dune Buggy Ent., 14850 Chestnut St., Westminster, California, 93001
Empi, Box 1120, Riverside, California, 92863
Fun Products, 2320 Auburn Blvd., Sacramento, California, 95821
John's Buggy Shop, 2112 Everett Ave., Everett, Washington, 98201
Kyote II, 3077 W. Cahuenga Blvd., Hollywood, California, 90028
Mangosta Sport Buggy, 57 E. Main, Ventura, California, 93001
Sport Buggies, 6660 Reseda Blvd., Reseda, California, 91335

Strictly German, 1025 W. 18th St., Costa Mesa, California, 92627

### West
Desert Fox, 1014 N. Central, Phoenix, Arizona, 85004
Fun Cars, Inc., 2132 E. 17th St., Tucson, Arizona, 85719
Linton Corp., Box 431, Sidney, Montana, 59270
The Scorpion, 1014 N. Central, Phoenix, Arizona, 85004

### Midwest
Automotive Fabrication, 4935 28th Ave., Rockford, Illinois, 61109
B-C Fiberglass Co., 885 Ennett St., Battle Creek, Michigan, 49017
Bremen Speed Equipment, Box 1, U.S. 6 East, Bremen, Indiana, 46506
Gary's Bug House, 106 W. Lake St., Minneapolis, Minnesota, 55408
Hartford Mfg. Co., 1051 Clinton St., Slinger, Wisconsin, 53086
J & R Enterprises, 1615 Oak Ave., Evanston, Illinois, 60201
Major Cars, Inc., 3626 Montrose Ave., Chicago, Illinois, 60018
Moka Plastics, 2551 N. Washington, Kokomo, Indiana, 46901
Phil's Auto Top, 2204 Ashland Ave., Evanston, Illinois, 60202
Sand Pounders, Inc., 516 N. Milwaukee Ave., Wheeling, Illinois, 60090

### East
B & D Speed Shop, 244 Adams St., Newton, Massachusetts, 02158
Cor Frames, Box 337, Villanova, Pennsylvania, 19085
D & C Automotive Industries, Box 371, Ridgefield, New Jersey, 07660
Dearborn Automobile Co., 2 Barnard St., Marblehead, Massachusetts, 01945
Fibre-Trend, 7 Grassy Plain St., Bethel, Connecticut, 06801
Fulton Eng. Co., 37 Vernon Blvd., Long Island City, New York, 11101
Irwin Equip., 1051 Clinton St., Buffalo, New York, 14206
Jackal Ent., 313 Bergen Turnpike, Ridgefield, New Jersey, 07660
Perfect Plastics, 1304 Third Ave., New Kensington, Pennsylvania, 15068

# 7. THE DUNE SCHOONER AND THE SWAMP BUGGY

*Dune schooner*

## THE DUNE SCHOONER

An offshoot of the dune buggy is the dune schooner, or dune scooter, which includes up to 5 bench seats for group cruising and sightseeing. It is a heavy-duty, specially built, modern vehicle with oversize tires for speeding over rolling sand dunes. A low center of gravity makes the dune schooner tip-proof, and the soft sand dunes do little damage to the undercarriage, oil pan, and flywheel housing. The immovable nature of obstructions in mountain terrain precludes its use there.

The dune schooner speeding over undulating hills of sand and along a lakeshore gives a rollicking, kid-style experience. In the summer, it affords the lush beauty of long green views, and in autumn, panoramas of colored trees, and in both seasons, moonlight rides, picnics, and beach parties.

Mac Woods of Mears, Michigan pioneered, almost a half-century ago, this form of off-road recreation. He spent years in persistent struggle, experimenting with different body styles and engines, finally evolving something that looks like a cross between a jeep and a Mack truck, has 10 oversize tires, and is adequate to scramble the hills of Oceana sand dunes and slosh through the waters of Lake Michigan.

## THE SWAMP BUGGY

The need to get through boggy ground, often wooded, heavily and highly grassed, and sometimes under water up to 10 inches, was probably the reason for the swamp buggy's creation. The cypress swamps and Everglades of Florida, the bayou country of the south-central states, and lands adjoining the coastal marshes represent some areas of use. There are no commercial models available, and as no particular style dominates, and no standards are apparent, the garage mechanic has no guidelines or restrictions in creating his swamp buggy. The sky is the limit.

**History** The swamp buggy's origin is difficult to substantiate, but Florida's pioneer was Ed Frank, who constructed (circa 1912) one out of an old Model T Ford chassis, and attached a set of oversize truck tires. It literally floated across the creeks and lagoons with all the muck in between. Living on the edge of the Everglades and interested in hunting, Ed was able to penetrate and probe the remote recesses of the Glades, heretofore known only to the Seminole Indians, alligators, and wild hogs.

ABOVE: The "buggy generation" uses this vehicle on hills, deserts, mountains, beaches, and sand dunes.

BELOW: Some buggies are austere by their lack of superstructure, but this arrangement gives better traction on difficult terrain.

*Super-wide, high-flotation tires give a soft ride, along with increased traction.*

**Modern Buggy** Following Ed Frank's concept, early swamp-bound outdoorsmen continued to use the Model T truck with oversize tires for traction to the seldom-seen places. Then, at the end of World War II, the 4-WD GI truck, along with surplus bomber plane tires, came upon the scene and was used to good advantage—continuing to the present day. Further developments are constantly noticeable and include cleated tires, roll bars, frames cut down to various sizes, boat-type bodies to ward off water, large tractor-type wheels, and some sort of truck bed (large or small) to freight in all the passengers and cargo for the projects in mind. The nondescript vehicle, without fenders, bumpers, or mud guards, carrying high-riding passengers, its engine snorting to drive tires through molasses-like semiliquidity, and the cleats of tires throwing geometric mud cakes in the air, represents the swamp buggy in its element and underway.

**Swamp Buggy Uses** The swamp buggy gives opportunity for a unique experience; that of roaming a terrain seldom visited by man. In Florida, the swamp buggy driver can travel through a fairyland of flora that includes palmetto, saw grass, scrub pine, and exotic flowers. Alligators and rare birds can also be seen. The

ABOVE: *In the prairie states, the buggy jumps like a grasshopper.*

BELOW: *Competing in a slalom race*

TOP: *A modern swamp buggy being field-tested before it is taken to the remote recesses of the Florida Everglades (J. L. Norman photo)*

ABOVE: *Many buggy clubs include youth driving clinics in their program of activities.*

buggy is ideal for use in connection with hunting camps that are located deep in swampland areas. There the hunting is usually profitable for ducks and geese, deer, bear, raccoon, boar (wild hogs), and wild turkey. Fishing in isolated potholes also represents a prolific spot with no picnickers to infringe. These out-camps, with primitive structures constructed by groups of outdoorsmen, are used season after season, and the swamp buggy gets them there for enjoyable participation in the sport of their choice.

In emergency situations, such as lost children or adults, airplane crashes, airboat accidents, etc., the swamp buggy has been commandeered into action.

## THE SWAMP BUGGY'S IMPACT ON ECOLOGY

The poaching of fish and game is probably the most serious charge against the users of the swamp buggy. With this vehicle, it is possible to get into the wilderness, far from law-enforcing agents; to shoot and spear birds, animals, and fish out of season; and to bring them out under the cover of darkness.

Game taken illegally (out of season, or over the limit) includes deer and boar. Game shot indiscriminately includes bear, raccoon, fox, opossum, wildcat, and flying birds. Alligators represent the most lucrative poaching project.

In times of flooding, game animals (mostly deer) concentrate on the elevated hummocks of land and are easily discovered and flushed into the water by dogs. The hunter takes an advantageous stand at the edge of the hummock and easily shoots the animal attempting to swim away to safety.

In times of drought, because of the fire hazard, the swamp buggy should not be used.

Thus, we find that the swamp buggy has little adverse impact on the land. It is in the area of wildlife conservation that users must commit themselves.

*The Naples, Florida annual "Swamp Buggy Races" where shade tree mechanics push their vehicles through a mile of mud before thousands of spectators*
(J. L. Norman photo)

# 8. THE TRAILBIKE

Motorcycles have come a long way since America's first mass-produced cycle, the famed Indian. Born in 1905, its features included a 2-cycle engine, battery ignition, gravity-feed oil system, gas tank mounted on the rear fender. Starting was achieved by pedaling.

Today, a great, great grandson, the motorized bike for off-road travel, is offered in many styles: trailbikes, minibikes, and three-wheelers—all with specialized tires, sophisticated engineering, strong body construction, and efficient power plants that challenge drivers in many activities and service uses.

On the vacation highways of our country, one senses immediately the popularity of off-road bikes. They are loaded on (and in) trailers, vans, campers, station wagons, and various other styles of recreation vehicles headed for the backcountry. The driver and passengers, after reaching their planned destinations, mount their spirited 2-wheel steeds and maneuver them along paths to places that offer ideal locales for hobbies of their choice.

In an effort to accommodate the many trailbikers and minibikers, federal and state agencies have allocated riding areas for motorized trail scooters. A few leading states, with their mileage, are: California, 5,247; Idaho, 4,498; Utah, 2,944; Washington, 2,916; Oregon, 2,188; Colorado,

1,820; Arizona, 1,331; and New Mexico, 1,000. However, there are 21 states without any trail accommodations.

The trailbiker is quite unlike the highway driver of a big machine. He uses a smaller bike that is capable of doing mansized jobs for freedom, a change of pace and geography, and getting away from it all.

In dimension the trailbike can approach a full-size motorcycle, but the similarity ends there, for it is made exclusively to reach places inaccessible to pack animals or four-wheel vehicles. This rugged mountain goat, crossed with a bucking bronco, it seems, gets its versatility from knobby tires, a gutsy power plant, sturdy frame construction, front telescopic fork, a high exhaust pipe, high ground clearance, and a short wheelbase. It roves the countryside for a hundred miles or more on a gallon of gas.

A narrow lane, no path at all, steep hills with up to 60° slopes, snow, mud, or water—the trailbike negotiates them all. The sure-footed vehicle, disdaining speed, is for the man with a purpose: up a mountain, hitting the hot sand, sloshing through a swamp, reaching a seldom-fished trout pool, repairing fences on a big spread, or just going so far that no one will be there to infringe on a personal escape. The trailbiker identifies with the terrain in a way that the

*No path at all, steep hills, and mud, the trailbike negotiates them all—and affords personal escape too.*

automobile driver, insulated from the road by 2 tons of steel and glass, can never appreciate.

The motorized bike also enables the physically handicapped or those limited in health to enjoy the back-country. For the young and healthy, it makes possible longer trips into remote country in search of personal goals.

## SERVICE USES OF THE TRAILBIKE

The trailbike is in use for multiple functions in far-flung, exotic corners of the world.

In South America's Chilean Andes Mountains, a party of geologists took 2 Trail-Breakers on an exploration mission as high as 20,000 feet. Where there are no roads between villages in the Philippine Islands and the rainy season is long, nothing moves but a trailbike. It is also invaluable to missionaries for transporting medical supplies and other needs of the natives. On a small Philippine Island in southern Mindanao, a shepherd daily rides to the grazing fields to check on his flock of some 60,000 animals.

The Ministry of Animal Industry, Game and Fisheries in Uganda, one of the emergent African nations, purchased 20 Trail-Breakers for use in a livestock development project.

At Savoonga, Alaska on the rocky coastline of the Bering Sea, a school teacher uses his Trail-Breaker to pull a dogsled carrying his wife and 4 children and an 80-gallon water container to and from a spring a half-mile from his home. It seems that the trailbike, along with the snowmobile, has replaced the traditional dogsled in the north country.

A prospector in Whitehorse, Yukon Territory, Canada, driving the trailbike through mud up to 2′ deep, hauled out a small bull moose from a swamp. In the winter, he uses his bike to plow through the powdery snow, which is up to 18″ deep.

Hunters of big game range farther afield, increase their odds of success, and are able to pack out their game with trailbikes. One hunter hauled out a 503-pound rough-dressed bull elk in 2 loads over 1½ miles of soft snow.

The trailbike and the helicopter teamed up to do an exploration job for the Texas Gulf Sulphur's South American affiliate. The helicopter airlifted trailbikes and personnel over rough and desolate terrain.

## OFF-ROAD ADVENTURING

Trailbiking has been described as being "akin to the deer's leap in a forest glade" for the character of the terrain is transferred upward through the wheels, frame, handlebars, and seat to the rider, who can't help but identify with the natural terrain, as does the fisherman receiving the impulse of his catch's struggle through rod, reel, and line.

That any off-road trailbike project requires some discipline and knowledge is obvious. Enjoyment comes only from a trouble-free ride, and a few simple rules are in order:

1. Along the off-road trail, riders meet other people as well as domestic animals. Accord the courtesy of throttling down and working slowly past groups of hikers, picnickers, and campers. Upon meeting horseback riders, pull off to the

side, shut off the engine, and wait until they are out of hearing distance before you start up again. This also applies to range cattle, sheep, and horses, which easily spook and may stampede.

2. Don't drive extreme steep grades straight up; slant across them in a series of switchbacks to cut down the angle of ascent. Going straight up places strain on the bike and damages the trail, causing erosion.

3. Riding downhill, shift the weight to the rear, and allow the compression of the engine to help the braking process. The standing or semistanding position helps.

4. Riding uphill, the weight should be forward while standing on the foot pegs, arms flexed, and chin down toward the handlebars. Keep up the momentum of the bike with as much speed as conditions warrant.

5. When driving over logs, over downed branches, or across deep ruts, it is best to approach them squarely, keeping the weight rearward, off the front wheel. An upward tug of the handlebars helps to ease the front wheel up and over tricky obstacles.

6. Driving through deep sand, wet leaves, or mud requires the shift of weight to the rear, permitting the drive tire to dig in for more traction. Don't race the motor so long as there is some forward motion, as speed under such conditions can result in a fall.

7. When driving parallel to the top of steep grades, keep the bike as vertical as possible by shifting your weight and maintain a steady speed. Keep the front wheel from turning to the downhill side and picking up speed.

8. Stream crossings call for driver caution, with the weight to the rear (for traction) and a watchful eye for submerged rocks, while traveling at a slow, steady speed. Keep the carburetor, wiring, and engine above water. Probably best, is to probe the water's depth by wading, and if it's too deep, carry the bike across.

9. Loose rocks are best approached with slow speed, keeping weight rearward and avoiding

*Hunters of big game range farther afield with a trailbike.*

the large ones. Loose rocks that spin away from the rear tire causing the bike to swerve sideward are the most dangerous.

10. In low brush and tall grass cruising, protect the feet by keeping them well back on the foot pegs; otherwise, such projections can catch and bend the foot down and back, which over a long trail can be quite irritating and painful.

11. Low bridges in the form of branches, fences, or guy wires require a bent-over-the-handlebars position, head down to protect the neck, face, and eyes.

12. Trails may be dusty; carry along a rag (in a plastic bag) for cleaning exposed parts—chains, sprockets, axles, etc.

13. Oil liberally all moving parts.

14. Even though tool kits are standard with most bikes, before off-road riding, check for wrenches, screwdrivers, pliers, etc., that properly fit all parts.

## TRAILBIKE CARE

All mechanical devices require constant attention such as lubrication, greasing, and tightening to prevent wear to moving parts and to keep all systems functioning properly. Although the modern trailbike is more endurable than earlier models, its rougher treatment requires constant attention, especially when it is used on extensive, off-road trips, where servicing facilities are not to be found.

The dealer's checkup, including complete inspection, tune-up, modifications, etc., is a preventive measure that guards against the probability of small problems developing into major ones. The checkup should include lubrication; check of spoke wiring; chain and carburetor adjustment; tire inspection; air system and air cleaner servicing; valve, oil pump, and clutch adjustments; and suspension systems.

*If the truck can't get a crew to a trouble-shooting job, the trailbike will.*

Study the warranty, know your guarantees, and follow all recommended procedures.

## ORGANIZED TRAILBIKING

Many of the trailbike owners (over a million) in the United States are affiliated with some group that caters to their interests, as in the extension of a snowmobile club program that serves as a continuing organized activity during the summer months. This extension of the enjoyment of the sport is achieved by joining a club, where interaction with kindred riders leads to the sharing of experiences and working with a group for a cause.

As a newcomer to trailbiking, attend as a guest some local club meetings to determine which group emphasizes your area of interest. Should none qualify, or if there are no clubs in your area, the local cycle dealer is a good place to start. He will give you names of riders, offering you an opportunity to stir up interest, whether it be in social activities, extensive tripping, camping, off-road excursions, litter clean-up, or other service objective.

*The Rocky Mountain Trials Association* illustrates the advantage of belonging to an organized group to extend off-road experiences. The group sponsors a regular program of trials. The trial is not a race, but rather a test of man controlling his machine in varied conditions that require rider skill, judgment, endurance, mechanical ability, and courage. The trial route is spaced by several observation points, where judges grade the rider's ability to maintain complete control of his cycle.

Trials are held monthly at various locations in the mountains and are organized by different "trialmasters" who check the terrain for suitability and public land permit matters. A map indicating how to find the area of participation is included with the notice of trials. The events are generally held in ideal picnic country so that entire family groups can enjoy the outing.

The group is conservation-minded and co-operates with government agencies in protecting and defending recreational rights and privileges.

Should you, or your group, be far from the Rocky Mountains and wish information for a local trials project, write: Bill Brokaw, 1314 Fountain Creek Blvd., Colorado Springs, Colorado, 80906, or Cycle Center, 4595 E. Virginia Ave., Denver, Colorado, 80222.

## COMPETITIONS

A large segment of cyclists are gung-ho on hill climbing, endurance runs, cross-country, and straight racing—all exciting and specialized uses of the trailbike. As these activities are too specialized for universal participation, only a cursory review is offered here.

The American Motorcycle Association sponsors amateur competition, in which trophies are awarded, but no prize money is paid. In 1969, there were 5,148 amateur events, held in all parts of the country, with more than 165,000 rider entries.

*Amateur competition* is divided into two major categories: speed events and non-speed events, run either on courses laid out around deserted airport runways or on specialized road-racing circuits. These courses are usually between 1 and 5 miles in circumference.

*Scramble events* are the most popular form of amateur competition. They are held on a closed, graded, dirt course between ½ mile and 2 miles long, with left-hand and right-hand corners and usually have a jump.

*The Cross-Country Race* is the same as the scramble except that the course is not graded.

*The Hare and Hound Race* is run cross-country on natural terrain, with course markers and checkpoints. It is most popular in the western deserts where an event will often have several hundred riders starting at the same time.

*Ice races* are run on oval tracks up to ½ mile in circumference and laid out on frozen lakes. They are held mostly in the northernmost states bordering on Canada and are usually from December through February. Ice racing cycles are fitted with special tires and extended fenders for safety.

*Hillclimbs* pit the rider against the clock as he attempts to follow a straight, but rough, path up the side of a high, steep hill. The hills are so difficult that only a few machines will be able to get all the way to the top. 40° slopes on hillclimb courses are not unusual.

*The Enduro* is the most popular form of non-speed event. It is a cross-country run, over many difficult types of terrain, in which the rider must try to maintain a constant average speed (usually 24 mph to 30 mph). The rider's average speed is measured at checkpoints along the obstacle route, and he is penalized if he arrives at a checkpoint early or late.

*Trials* are held on a number of short sections of nasty, tricky terrain with obstacles marked with border tapes. The rider must try to cross each section, keeping both feet on the foot pegs, and he is scored by an observer along the route.

The amateur competition program, sponsored by the American Motorcycle Association, has been laid out with an eye toward offering something of interest to the experienced rider who wishes a more advanced type of activity.

## OTHER PROGRAM ACTIVITIES

There are many club activities that serve as ideal family outings.

*A Hare and Hound Chase* is a game in which the leader (hare) takes a head start and drops off small bags of lime along a zigzag course. The contestants (hounds) try to catch up without losing the trail. All enjoy a barbeque or picnic at the trail's end.

*Treasure Hunt* starts out by giving each participant a mimeographed sheet of instructions that lead bikers through various terrains as they decipher and follow the printed clues. Many prizes have been hidden en route, and the grand prize is at the end of the hunt. Cool drinks and food for all climax the activity.

*Public service* is engaged in by many clubs. This often leads to a better feeling in the community. The clean-up or anti-litter project represents a project where an entire club drives to a local park, picnic grove, or fishing banks and picks up the litter, sometimes soliciting community-owned trucks to help tote out the refuse.

The Pasadena (California) Motorcycle Club annually helps in the control of throngs of people at the famous Tournament of Roses pageant and Rose Bowl Game on New Year's Day.

Another California club stages an annual tour, the proceeds of which go to the City of Hope National Medical Center. Their 1970 gift was more than $2,500.

The Sports Committee of District 37, American Motorcycle Association, discovering that a hospital in Mojave, California, was $5,000 short of being able to open, assessed its racing members 25¢ per event over a half-year period, and accumulated and presented the necessary amount.

## CLUB-AGENCY COOPERATION

Slickrocking in Utah is an example of fostering trailbiking by cooperation among several groups: the Bureau of Land Management (Monticello District); Dick Wilson, who is an outdoor writer for the *Moab Times-Independent* and proposed it; and clubs which participate and whose members comport themselves in a sportsmanlike manner.

The term "slickrock" comes from an extensive formation of Navajo sandstone, which is characterized by its smooth, rolling surface and lack of growing vegetation and is ideal for the low-geared nature of the trailbike, so that there is no destruction of landscape.

A practice trail of 2.3 miles and a 10.3 mile trail for experienced drivers are included. The aims of both are being non-competitive and riding for the enjoyment of sightseeing the buff-colored sliprock formations, which look as if they were poured in gentle undulation, then solidified into smooth ramps and hills. The surface offers ideal traction for motorized vehicles as they cruise along sandstone rims where many points offer sweeping views of the rocky country, including Arches National Monument. Then, the route drops 600 feet to the Colorado River. The nature-paved trail is an ideal terrain for trailbiking since the government bureau gives its blessing and the hospitable town welcomes visitors, and clubs react by injuring neither the land nor their own public image.

## ASSOCIATIONS

For additional information on individual, group, and club activities, racing, and service outlets, write:

American Motorcycle Assoc., 5655 N. High St., Worthington, Ohio, 43085

American Desert Racing Assoc., Box 3189, Westminster, California, 92683

National Off-Road Racing Assoc., 1616 Victory Blvd, Glendale, California, 91201

The Golden Circle Assoc., Box 111, Moab, Utah, 84532

## TRAILBIKE CAMPING

Gaining popularity is the week-end campout in the desert, mountains, or woods with a trail-

LEFT: *The sand stretch of an Enduro Race.*

*Slickrock country affords sweeping views of the rugged landscapes.*

bike that has the power to take heavy loads and campers a bit farther, and where the fishing's better and the campsites are ample. Perhaps the backpacker, mountain climber, or hiker may look down on you, but it is great for the older camper who cannot hike the way he used to, or when your time is short and you wish to go far into the hinterland, pack out big game, or find some rumored treasure.

You may need to sling a pair of haversacks astride the bike frame, a packsack on the rear rack, and one on your back. Obviously, a pack on your back while riding will affect balance, so before hitting the trail, practice in the backyard with the unnatural load on your back.

THE TRIP PLAN

The trail of travel, whether on National Forest, state land, private ranch, or abandoned roads,

should first be checked out for driving conditions, the best starting point, possible rest stops en route, the campsite, and return route. Check with local authorities about the water supply, availability of firewood, regulations, and posted areas for motorized vehicles. One experienced driver who has been over the trail should act as the "trailmaster."

Outdoorsmen who have evolved camping lists over the years must consider anew many modes of operation for a trailbiking campout. Your gear will be similar to that of a backpacker, who carries his house on his back. Cut down the cooking kit to a minimum of pots and utensils. Paper plates and cups should be considered, as they are light, and can be burned after use. The cooking fire will be over available wood, or perhaps, a one-burner camp stove that packs conveniently.

**Food** A few canned foods may be considered

such as stews, certain fruits, and vegetables. Even fresh meat can be taken for the first evening meal. It is best, however, to stay with the lightweight foods: dehydrated, freeze-dried, powdered, and dry—which are nutritional and flavorful. Also, consider dry fruit, dry soups in foil packages, beef jerky, bacon bars, and margarine, which keeps better than butter. Hopefully, there'll be fish to augment the food supply, but do not depend on it. On long trips it is a good idea to use up the heaviest foods first, to lighten the load as the trip progresses. With youngsters in the group, take along a liberal supply of chocolate bars, nuts, hard candy, and/or energy bars. If there is a need for a nip of bourbon for adult campers at the end of the day, an anodized aluminum flask will carry it best.

**Shelter** A mountain, pup, or pop tent is recommended. A plastic sheet or ground tarp, grommeted at the corners and sides for erection between two trees, represents another type of lightweight shelter. For a ground cloth (moisture barrier) use a poncho or plastic sheet, then place the bedroll on it. Pitch the tent on a slight grade for drainage without digging trenches. Place the entrance away from the prevailing wind and away from large trees, but in the protection of some brush cover.

**Clothing** Considerations should include sturdy leg-hugging trousers, long sleeved shirts, a windbreaker, sturdy shoes, and a helmet with a visor. Take along a change of underclothes, pants, and shirt in case of a drenching rain. Also include sun glasses and ditty bag for personal items. Sleeping bags should be highly compressible and suitable for the region.

**Packing** Use straps or webbing instead of rope, which will chafe in lashing down all the gear to the bike. Your trailbike will carry 250 pounds or more, so the balancing of the cargo is important. Be sure to include such easily forgotten items as waterproof matches, flashlight, first-aid kit, compass, map of the area, flares, extra gas, tire pump, and tool kit.

**En route to the Campsite** Once at the embarkation-point, check with local authorities about trail conditions, prohibited lands, possible problem areas, fire regulations, etc. Once underway, you will need to focus all your attention on the trail and obstacles such as brush, low-hanging branches, boulders, windfalls, and water hazards. If you need a candy bar or chewing gum for a pick-me-up, stow the wrappers in your

pocket and burn them at the campsite. If your trip involves fording a stream, make sure that it is shallow enough for the ignition wires and engine to clear.

One plan for trailbiking camping includes a drop-off of machines, gear, and drivers by truck or trailer at some distant point, then camping and driving back home. Another requires driving first to the rendezvous, camping, and being picked up by truck, train, or bus. This way there is no backtracking a familiar route.

After a long stretch at the wheel, take a break, especially during the heat of the day. Walk the last few yards up a mountain crest, to a lake or stream for scenic views. Don't drive the very

*This Colorado off-roader leaves the bike, and hikes to a strategic position to photograph the Black Canyon.*

*Joining a club offers opportunity for off-road experiences.*

last inch; that way you'll enjoy the change of pace, use different muscles, and disrupt less. Cooling off the machine and rider in the shade, or taking off your shoes and wading in a stream also makes good sense. Keep the pace leisurely. Don't inject the rush element into the project.

When you meet others on the trail, pull off and stop to give plenty of leeway for them to pass. Be careful of gouging paths with spinning tires that later will be further eroded by wind and rain. Leave all gates, either opened or closed, as you found them.

**The Campsite** Make camp in plenty of time to set up the shelter, cook the evening meal, wash the dishes, and enjoy the twilight hours. Should

the water supply be questionable, carry canteens or water bags. Halzone tablets or boiling water can provide safe water.

Kitchen wastes from foodstuffs of organic matter will decompose readily, however, burn as much as possible. Don't bury your garbage, as bears and other animals have lots of time to find it, dig it up, and strew it about.

Bring water for dishes to the kitchen area and wash and rinse all utensils, pots, and pans there rather than at the lake or streamside. Soap and detergents, fish entrails, garbage, and trash should never be disposed of in any body of water. Hard litter such as cans, bottles, foil, oil cans, and other unburnable refuse, must be packed out.

Where there are no toilet facilities, agree on a site well away from any type of water, other camping areas, and trail. Dig a hole or trench and backfill with dirt after each use. Should the group be large and the stay long, the latrine should include a supply of dehydrated lime, which is sprinkled over the dirt to cut down on odors and keep away flies.

The trailbikes should be put away for the night by setting them up on their stands, away from the kitchen area or paths of travel about the campsite. Cover them with ponchos or tarps for protection against dampness. Wood for the morning fire can also be stored under the tarps.

At the end of your back-country jaunt, clear the campsite so that no evidence of your stay is obvious. Take out more litter than you brought. Vow that no one will have to take out your garbage. Common sense and good manners enhance the image of trailbiker campers—and it needs all the help it can get.

**Leave No Trace** Mr. G. A. Cunningham of Outdoor Sports Industries, Denver, Colorado, 80216, and columnist for *Better Camping* magazine, is a veteran mountain backpacker and canoeist, and has written "How to Camp—and Leave No Trace." The booklet should be the bible for those who trod wild places. Chapter headings such as "The Ethics of Camping, Modes of Travel that Leave no Trace," "How to Sleep in the Wilderness and Leave no Trace," "Wilderness Shelters that Leave no Trace," and "How to Use Fire and Leave no Trace" all lead up to the Wilderness Traveler's Creed:

I believe that man—the intelligent animal—can travel through the wilderness and leave no trace.
I will keep my group small.
I will keep my stay in one place short.
I will not cut down trees or branches.
I will not build fires, or if I do I will keep them small and scatter their remains when I leave.
I will leave no trash or other evidence of my stay in the wilderness.
I will leave no trace.

The adventure-bent trailbiker, experiencing that out-of-the-way rendezvous, should realize a code of good conduct must be followed. With the ever-increasing use of off-road vehicles and the decrease of available land, trailbikers, as all off-road travelers, must make some concessions in order to preserve the lands now being used and to gain more areas in the future.

The practical off-roader wishes to equate his bike with utility and adventure along with fun, not as a chromed, fur-seated status symbol that sits most of the time on the front lawn or driveway. The trailbike need not be the fastest, most ornate, or most expensive vehicle; it simply fills the bill for the individual's own ambitions and experiences.

## THE SELECTION OF YOUR BIKE

1. Seek out a good dealer who will test-drive, check, and tune-up the cycle before delivery. Without such attention, you may have to return after a few days of driving with complaints on clutch, sprockets, tires, throttle, timing, etc.

2. At the shop, watch the mechanic work on your cycle. Most dealers are happy when customers learn to make minor adjustments and simple repairs.

3. Keep to the warranty check-up schedule.

4. Take in the bike with your problems written out.

## THE TRAILBIKE'S IMPACT ON ECOLOGY

Opponents of motorized vehicles challenge the off-road driver to walk with them, to gaze upward to observe the hawk soaring on rising thermals in the sky, to look down to the forest floor at a barely visible flower or mushroom pushing its way through dead leaves or pine needles, a deer browsing but a few yards away, and the sweeping panorama with multiple textures and colors. The devotee of the walk claims that these sights are never available to the rider astride his bike, prodding the hot and noisy machine, speeding along with eyes intent only on the road. They indict the trailbiker and minibiker as hot rodders in the woodland who dig up slopes, destroy delicate vegetation, spook wildlife, and disturb the peace of feathered and furred creatures as well as humans. Also, they mention the fire hazard potential that is increased in wooded and field areas of participation, especially in periods of drought and in the late summer.

In 4 California counties (Los Angeles, Orange, San Bernardino, and Riverside) laws are in effect banning all motorbikes from public or private property without written consent by the owner.

However, a more recent state law may preempt the local ordinances, in effect invalidating them.

In Southern California, thousands of trailbikers take to the desert and mountains every weekend, and outnumber hikers and horseback riders by hundreds to one. The ecologists feel that the motorized recreational vehicles are destroying the desert, even though before their onslaught, ten or so years ago, it was considered useless.

The trailbikers counter with the observation that the springtime flash floods and numerous sand storms do infinitely more damage. As a trailbiker, you know that your mount weighs significantly less than a packhorse and most other vehicles, and that a group of careless hikers, a string of burros, or even a horse and wagon can scar the land much more than a trailbike.

The off-road bike's design of large tires, weight of less than 300 pounds, and low horsepower limits its potential for destruction. The driver can deftly avoid saplings and delicate growth with a slight turn of the handlebars. Littering by trailbike operators offers a small problem, mainly because there is limited cargo space.

Ecologist David Plourde indicates that, "A bulldozer dragging half a dozen logs through the woods to a loading platform makes a mess that no thirty bikes could match in a month." Another ecologist, Larry Gann, states in a report excerpted from the *Arkansas Gazette*, ". . . the properly geared and tired trailbike will be less damaging to a trail than a horse."

While the trailbike is inherently non-destructive, it can adversely affect the environment and, like all mechanical devices, it should be used prudently with reason and respect. Education, not restriction, is the answer. Responsible and courteous usage of the machine can succeed in convincing others that the motorized bike is not a vehicle that has an irreversible impact on the environment. Trailbikes, as any motorized recreational vehicle, do not destroy the land, but those who steer them may. The problem is compounded, of course, by sheer numbers and unthinking participants. As for most problems created by new vehicles, the basic solution rests with the personal use and sense of responsibility of the individuals involved.

The problems of trailbiking represent another manifestation of over-population, the flocking habit of man, the artificial living, and in an attempt to escape these pressures, the participant is vulnerable on many fronts.

* From *Colorado Outdoors* magazine, July, 1968.

After all, many individuals possess some form of motorized bike. They come in a wide spectrum of age-span, intelligence, motivations, and judgement. A small number will transgress and their indiscretions are magnified. If you gave that segment of participants pogo sticks, wouldn't the same minority get into trouble?

Many of my good city-oriented friends, echoing anti-vehicle proclamations, without ever experiencing the use of one or the observation of delinquencies by vehicle operators, are answered, "Look, you and I buy a trailbike, a snowmobile, a 4-WD vehicle, or an ATV, and use it extensively. I'm sure that neither you nor I would ever desecrate the land, or bother a soul, or harm wildlife! Don't you think the majority of people are like us?"

The following guidelines, applicable to all off-road vehicles, can insure conservation of the outdoors and responsibility toward others:

1. Remember wild, wilderness, and primitive areas are closed to motorized vehicles including trail machines.

2. Motorized vehicles and trailbikes are to be used only on established roads and parking areas in national parks and monuments.

3. Areas which are restricted for motorized vehicle travel due to fire hazards, recent seedings or plantings, domestic watershed, etc., are not to be entered.

4. Do not enter private property without permission of the owner.

5. Bypass or avoid water bars or earth bars which are placed to arrest erosion. Trail machines should be lifted over such barriers if they are encountered.

6. Practice good fire prevention rules and do not litter the trails.

7. Avoid trails which would take the trailbike through soft meadows, loose top soils, steep hills, or freshly seeded terrain. This practice will avoid erosion of soil or damage to new seedlings. Do not spin the drive wheel.

8. Do not disturb isolated water holes used by wild game and livestock, campers or fishermen.

9. Never shoot from any vehicle—trailbikes included.

10. Remain on established trails, paths, and roadways for an enjoyable trip. This avoids damage to soil and terrain and disturbance to fellow sportsmen. *

No doubt you became an off-roader with a motorized vehicle through interests in fishing, hunting, camping, hiking, or some other pursuit; therefore, it should be easy to identify with others' points of view—the hunter who requires silence, the hiker who attains his goal through hard sweaty labor, or the camper who seeks remote areas for solitude.

The basic values for the off-roader lie in the identification with the natural environment, the understanding of its problems, and the expansion of experimental and philosophical horizons—always leaving the growing delicate things as you found them, or better.

## BUYER'S GUIDE

Entrees in the trailbike field are many, and all manufacturers have their own contribution to offer.

**Rokon, Inc.** (160 Emerald St., Keene, New Hampshire, 03411) offers three Trail-Breaker models available from dealers, as far north as Savoonga, on St. Lawrence Island, southwest of Nome, Alaska. This is Rokon's most remote dealer and here trailbikes, along with snowmobiles, have replaced the traditional dogsled team for tundra, hill, rocky country, and snow travel.

The Trail-Breaker fulfills a long-standing need for a mechanized, remote-area type of transportation. Features include an automatic clutch, 9 hp engine, independent front- and rear-wheel power, high ground clearance of 15", oversized tires that exert less force per square inch than a man on foot, dual starting system, and kick and rope pull. The trailbike fords streams up to 24" deep or can be floated in deeper water. The 4 to 5-pound air pressure in the tires absorbs shocks. The vehicle scampers over logs 28" in diameter, and negotiates grades up to 60°. That the Trail-Breaker may sink to a depth of 12" in mud and still be able to maintain a constant forward motion without necessitating any manhandling is due to its 2-wheel drive, the oversized and cleated wheels, and the elimination of the need for hand clutching. These remote-area bikes come in three models: MK-III, MK-IV, and Rokon Trail 140.

Price: $695 and up.

Options: front cargo rack, water-tight tool box, rear tow bar, emergency tool and spare parts kit, bumper rack, rustless chain, and rear passenger kit.

**American Honda Motor Co., Inc.** (Box 50-100 W. Alondra Blvd., Gardena, California, 90247), with the largest dealer network in the United States, offers

*Trail-Breaker*

the Scrambler 100 with its powerful 4-stroke engine, capable of 66 mph on the open road, sweptback tailpipe, and above average gas mileage. The Motosport 100 is characterized by power and lightness that enable it to churn through mud and climb steep grades. The Motosport 175, with its 5-speed transmission, 4-stroke twin engines, and sturdy "V" frame, is ideal for off-road use.

Price: $495.

**Kawasaki Motors Corp.** (1062 McGaw Ave., Santa Ana, California, 92705) and **Eastern Kawasaki** (3 Production Way, Avenel, New Jersey, 07001), a Japanese late comer on the U.S. scene, offer the Trail Boss with its 11.5 hp, double-loop tube frame and automatic oil injection, with a 12,000-mile or 12-month warranty.

Price: $485; Competition Scrambler, $669.

**Indian Motorcycles, Inc.** (1535 W. Rosecrans Ave., Gardena, California, 90249), offers the Bobcat 100, geared to the professional sportsman with its high-speed stability and its ease of handling over the roughest terrain. Also offered is the Competition Scrambler, which features a telescopic fork front and hydraulic swing arm, rear suspension, and a 12.5 hp engine.

Price: $449.

**Tote Gote Industries, Inc.** (225 East 9th South, Box 58, Provo, Utah, 84601), offers the Tote Gote

750, a 7 hp trailbike, featuring ease of operation and a minimum of maintenance; and the Tote Gote 780, a 7 hp cycle with climb-away transmission which adjusts automatically to load and speed, and hand-operated controls. Tote Gote was the champion machine of the National Trail Scooter Association in 1967, 1968, and 1969, over 12 to 30 miles of the roughest cross-country race course.

Price: Tote Gote 750, $479.95; Tote Gote 780, $489.95.

**Suzuki Motors Corp.** (13767 Freeway Drive, Santa Fe Springs, California, 90670), another Japanese firm, offers in its line of 14 models some ideal trail-bikes. Among them are the TS-125R Duster, with a 5-speed transmission, kick starter, a tripmeter, and a tachometer; the TS-185R Sierra with 3-way adjustable front forks, 5-way adjustable rear shocks, and great climbing ability; and the TS-250R Savage, with competition-type expansion chamber exhaust, pointless electronic ignition which keeps plugs from fouling, and high performance engine which has won many races. A 12-month or 12,000-mile warranty covers every major component of all bikes.

Price: Duster, $495; Sierra, $599; Savage, $799.

**Rupp Industries, Inc.** (1776 Airport Road, Mansfield, Ohio, 44903), offers at the top of the line the Roadster 2, with 12" wire spoke wheels and knobby tires designed to grip off-road surfaces. It can be modified with front and rear lights for street use where legal. The Black Widow model is a racing machine designed specifically for off-road competition. It's a big bike in feel and appearance, appealing to cyclists who want a specialized competition machine.

Price: Roadster 2, $309; Black Widow, $329.

TOP: *Mini-Enduro*
ABOVE: *Sport 5-30*

LEFT: *Screamer*
BELOW: *Dynamo Woodbike*

**Yamaha International Corp.** (Box 6600, Buena Park, California, 90620) is second only to Honda in total sales. They concentrate on trailbikes, which account for 75 percent of their production. The Mini-Enduro is powered by a 4½ hp, valve inducted, single cylinder, 2-stroke engine and includes a 4-speed gearbox with a hand clutch. Other features include a steel frame in double down tube configuration, stainless steel fenders, and a comfortable seat. It is also lightweight (121 pounds).
Price: $299.

**Arctic Enterprises, Inc.** (Box 635, Thief River Falls, Minnesota, 56701) offers the Screamer, which is powered by a Chrysler 8 hp engine. The transmission is snowmobile-type torque converter, the knobby tires measure 14" x 6", and suspension is telescopic fork in the front and swing arm in the rear. The machine weighs 94 pounds and has a ground clearance of 7".
Price: $289.95.

**Coleman Co. Inc.** (250 N. St. Francis, Wichita, Kansas, 67201) lists the Sport 5-30 for wilderness and high country travel. Extras for this model include internal expanding brakes, 10" wire spoke wheels, front and rear suspension, a 5-speed foot shift, and a 5.3 hp Sachs engine. A 2.40 model is also available.
Price: Sport 5-30, $369.95; 2.40 model, $297.95.

**Cosmopolitan Motors, Inc.** (Jacksonville & Meadowbrook Aves., Hatboro, Pennsylvania, 19040 —U.S. importers and distributors of Benelli Italian cycles) offers the Dynamo Woodbike with a strong, quiet engine. Its folding handlebars promise a comfortable ride for the tall rider.
Price: $329.

**Gill Manufacturing Co. Inc.** (3507 N. Kenton Ave., Chicago, Illinois, 60641) presents the Trail Hawk with a 7 hp engine and 2-speed automatic transmission, which make it ideal for travel in mud, ice, snow, weeds, sand, and grass. It fits into a car trunk for easy transportation. Price: $270.

**Yankee Motor Co.** (323 W. Alondra, Gardena, California, 90247 and Box 36, Schenectady, New York, 12301) is a distributor for the Ossa 250 Pioneer Enduro that is manufactured in Spain. The bike, intended for off-road use, includes a skid pan underneath to protect the engine and transmission from boulders, rocks, and logs, along with a thickly-padded saddle seat for 2 and buddy foot pegs. Other features include a single cylinder, 2-stroke engine; front tire size of 3" x 21" and rear tire, 4" x 18"; clutch-operated 5-speed transmission; overall length of 83.5"; seat height of 31"; and ground clearance of 9.5". Price: in New York, $930.

**Steen's, Inc.** (1635 West Valley Blvd., Box 2276, Alhambra, California, 91803) offers the Taco 102, a 6½ hp trailblazer geared to give safe, responsible performance to plow through a jungle of mud or desert wash with adequate maneuverability; the Taco Super 100, a "go anywhere" trailbike that is still tame enough for any member of the family to ride; and the Taco Trail, with dependable power, easy handling, and safe driving qualities. All models have Tecumseh engines and Mercury clutches. Price: Taco 102, $299; Super 100, $199.50; Trail, $189.50.

**Huron Tool and Manufacturing** (6554 S. Lake Shore Road, Lexington, Michigan, 48450) offers El Burro, strictly off-road cycles, and in the 5 and 8 hp class, Briggs & Stratton, 4-cycle engines. Features include 2 huge 12" x 30" tires, which take the rider through field, wood, desert, and mountains; fold-down handlebars; welded steel tube frame; heat-treated wear components; and dust seals on needle and ball bearings.
Price: El Burro, $349; Torque 5, $389.95; and Super 8, $399.95.

TOP: *Trail Hawk*
ABOVE: *Super 100*
RIGHT: *El Burro*

# 9. THE MINIBIKE

Two million minibikes, being driven in back-yards, in off-road areas, and on special trails, are evidence of a compatible vehicle for adults and young people, who emulate parents and older brothers and sisters by buying and asking for a minibike as a gift.

## DEFINITION OF A MINIBIKE

According to the Motorcycle Industry Council, to classify as a mini a vehicle must have less than a 10″ wheel diameter, less than 40″ wheelbase, less than 45 cc engine, and less than 25″ seat height, measured at the lowest point of the seat cushion without a rider. Most of the manufactured models, however, do not meet these standards.

Another deliberately loose definition is: a bike powered by a 4-cycle industrial engine of 2 to 6 hp with tire diameter of 11″ to 17″ and without specifications as to transmission, brakes, suspension, height, or frame.

*Minibike World Magazine's* definition is, "A minibike is any mechanically self-propelled, 2-wheeled vehicle except those described as 'scooters,' having a wheel rim diameter not exceeding 10″.

## THE VERSATILE VEHICLE

Regardless of the nuances in definition, the minibike is usually a "second" play bike. It is small enough and lightweight enough to fit neatly inside a station wagon, to be attached to the rear of a car or camper bumper, or to be transported to the riding fields or trails "broken down" in the car trunk.

The recreationist drives his vehicle as far as the road permits, parks, mounts the 2-wheeler and drives to more remote and roadless areas: the trout fisherman to that hidden lake; the explorer with his Geiger counter, metal detector, or geologist's pick to some promising rock formations; the prospector to a likely looking stream to pan for gold; the naturalist to a potentially rewarding tract with microscope and binoculars; or the urban dweller to the beckoning field and forest in search of pure air and the sounds of nature.

The yachtsman hauls his minibike aboard, unloads it at a port or other interesting locale for shopping, exploring, and other activities.

Farmers and ranchers inspect their land and round up stray stock, driving their minibikes over rough fields and rolling land.

In some states, the minibike becomes a legal highway bike with the addition of a horn and lights.

## CHARACTERISTICS OF A MINIBIKE

There are no definite criteria that adequately

*The minibike is usually a second play bike.*

define a minibike, but many general characteristics are recognized. Motors range from the simple souped-up lawn mower-type (2 hp), enabling the rider to reach speeds of 10 to 15 mph over level ground, to the refined engineering models (5.55 hp), having four gears and a manual clutch, with a top speed of 50 mph.

A minibike, selling for approximately $100 (total weight usually a shade over 60 pounds), is constructed of a simple tubular steel frame, a plain seat with no springs to cushion the ride, friction brakes in which a flat piece of steel rubs against the tire rim when the brake pedal is activated, and a hand-operated throttle on the handlebars. The small motor starts with a pull of the starting cord. No electric start is offered, even as an accessory.

In the $300 price tag class are models with detachable or folding handlebars, leak-proof gas caps, two-wheel brakes, kick starters, small motorcycle motors with transmissions containing 2 to 5 speeds, and an automatic shift or motorcycle-type hand clutch.

Ranging in price up to $500, in weight up to 200 pounds, higher priced models have increased engine horsepower, sturdier frames, shock-absorbing springs, simulated animal skin seat coverings, bright paint and chrome, bigger tires, better brakes, headlights, and reflectors.

## BUYING YOUR MINIBIKE

Base your selection of a bike on common-sense principles:

*The folding minibike makes storage and transportation a lot easier.*

1. Proper size and power.
2. Your experience driving a motorized bike.
3. Your ability to handle the machine you propose to buy.
4. The specific use you plan to make of the bike.
5. Actually sit on the model you expect to buy in order to check for comfort in the seating position, the leg room, etc.
6. Don't be affected by dazzling chrome and ornate appointments.
7. If possible, take a trial spin.

As to the final selection, remember that there is a wide range of minibike models from many companies—whose turnover, incidentally, is quite high, some dropping out, others constantly entering the field. Invest your money in a bike from a company that you feel will be around for a long time, will back up their product, and will supply parts, when needed.

If you ride a bicycle, learning to drive a motorized mini isn't difficult but practice in the backyard or on a field, not on pavement.

Don't tackle tricky hills too soon, for on steep grades, with the front wheel losing contact with the ground, you may flip backward—in motorized bike parlance, do a "wheelie."

Don't forget a helmet, insurance, and proper apparel, and after reading the manual, stick to the maintenance schedule.

Accessories are available for all minibikes. Your local dealer or manufacturer will fill you in on what's available for your model, along with prices. Accessories are numerous and include windshield, electric start, rearview mirrors, squeeze (bulb-type) and electric horns, saddle bags, luggage rack, basket, tool and repair kit, speedometer, gas gauge, T-shirts, and helmets.

## ORGANIZED PARTICIPATION

The American love affair with wheels is best illustrated in California, where its popularity is greatest, passing that of Little League baseball and junior football programs.

The Los Angeles YMCA, in a pilot program of minibiking, discovered that previously incorrigible youngsters made better students for the reward of participation in supervised events. And the police realize that a youngster is better off riding in a controlled program than sitting around, bored and waiting for excitement.

In an effort to extend controlled participation, Dr. Edwin Staley, State Director of Recreation and Youth Services Planning Council for the county of Los Angeles, recommends that the county develop areas in city parks and other public locations for motorized bikes of low horse-power.

At Point Mugu, near Los Angeles, a series of family-oriented vehicle riding trails is being developed which will represent a first in the state park system.

The officials of Orange County are considering a 24-acre cycle park along the Santa Ana River in Anaheim.

Costa Mesa has many motorized bike clubs for boys 16 and under, designed to keep the young-sters and their bikes off the streets, playgrounds, and parks.

Near Ukiah, bike riders have been using, in a controlled program, Bureau of Land Manage-ment fire-breaks as riding trails with little, if any, damage.

Saddleback Park, in Southern California, has been serving the bike riders for almost a decade,

*Instructions to minibike racers and spectators*

## Rally Officials and Their Duties

**Starter:** Makes sure course is clear, checks the timer for readiness. Makes sure proper contestant is ready. Give signal: "Ready, Go" (on 60 drop the flag). When contestant finishes his run, drop flag again, and instruct contestant to return to waiting area.

**Timer:** Take the contestant's blue slip, check his number on the helmet. Start watch on "Go", stop watch at the second flag drop. Record the time on the slip after checking with the field judges. Give slip to the runner.

**Runner:** Recieve the blue time slips from the timer, take them, one at a time to the recorder sitting at the table in front of the bathouse. Return to the timer's side for the next slip. Be in charge of the first aid kit.

**Recorder:** Record the times on both your blue sheets and the blackboard. Be sure your figures agree. Retain the blue time slips in your metal box.

**Inspection:** Check over each bike according to the printed rules and use your own judgement. If in doubt you may want to test the bike yourself. Of those that you pass, give them a pink slip, instruct them to take their bike to the waiting area and then to present their pink slip to the registration desk.

**Registration:** After a contestant gives you his pink slip and the fee, ($1.00 for Y-members, $2.00 for non-members), take his name and the necessary information on the master sheet. Assign him a number and instruct him to tape it to the back of his helmet and return to the waiting area. Be sure to give him two time slips and tell him to present them to the starter when he is called.

**Waiting Area Supervision:** Keep all bikes in the waiting area. Be ready to send out the next contestant when the starter calls for him. You may permit bike to go to the Parking lot for repairs if necessary.

**Spectator Area Supervision:** Keep all spectators, youths and adults in the spectator's area. (Also contestants who are not in the waiting area). Be sure that no spectators wonder onto the course.

**Gate Intrance Supervision:** Pass out the green sheets to all arriving persons. Tell contestants with bikes to go to the inspection area and spectators to go to the spectator area.

**Field Judges:** B sure each hazard in your area is set as it should be before each run. Keep your eyes on the bike and rider at all times. No contestant should ever be out of sight of all field judges. After each run signal the Starter according to the number of 'faults' the contestant had. Signal the Starter in case of an emergancy or injury. You may assist any contestant by giving directions etc.

We will try to take a 15-minute break between the two heats to evaluate and correct any problems arising in the first heat.

At the end of the second heat the Starter will announce the winners in front of the bathouse. We appreciate all of you coming out to help and hope that you will stay and help clean up the grounds.

## TO ALL MINI-BIKE CONTESTANTS AND SPECTATORS
### WELCOME

1— Take your bike to the inspection area to the left of the main gate. Your bike and you will be checked accordingly:

   1. Kill Switch necessary
   2. Feet must touch ground when sitting on bike
   3. Brakes must work
   4. No unusual smoke from exhaust, or engine leaks
   5. Bikes may be rejected because of sloppy maintenance if in the opinion of the Judge the fault may effect safety: Examples: Oil or grease near brakes, loose bolts, etc.

2— If your bike passes inspection, take it to the waiting area between the starting line and the bathouse. Then you go to the registration desk at the bathouse. Be sure to present your inspection slip. Fee for the rally is $1.00 for Y-members and $2.00 for non-members. You will recieve a numbered card which should be taped to the back of your helmet. Return to your bike but keep your bike in the confines of the waiting area.

3— At 10:30, or after the bikes have been registered, there will be a walk-through of the course to be sure you understand where the course goes. Late-arriving contest-ants will not get a walk-through but will have to ask for a "talk-through from the official starter before the first run.

4— Each contestant will have two runs: the worst time is dropped. Between runs all bikes must remain in the waiting area. Repairs may be made in the parking lot but only after permission is granted from the waiting area supervisor.

5— Depending on the number of entries, the rally may be divided according to age groups or horsepower groups. One trophy will be awarded for every 15 entries. Trophies may be picked up at the Y office on December 31st.

6— In running the course, no "hazard" can be avoided. Once the clock begins on a run it will keep turning. In event of mechanical difficulties on the first heat the contestant may scratch, fix the bike, and re-start if the second heat has not already begun. If such difficulties occur on the second heat, the contestant must be ready before the last rider has completed his second heat. In extreme cases, field judges may disqualify contestants. Contestants will recieve 2-second penalties for leaving the course or disturbing any of the course markers.

7— All spectators must remain in the viewing area reserved for them. No one will be permitted to walk on the course after the rally has begun.

*Rally Officials and their Duties*

and Gardena's Ascot Park Raceway is tailored for minibiking, with supervised and patrolled riding. Bikes are limited in horsepower, and drivers must wear protective clothing and helmets, and a notarized registration card for minors is required.

Throughout the state, cycle clubs are noted for their services: policing the public land on which they ride, engaging in litter pick-up rallies, and maintaining trails at their own expense.

Wisconsin is developing a network of trails that will serve off-road vehicles in the summer and snowmobiles in the winter. The first park is located near the capital at Madison and will in-clude campgrounds, picnic areas, rally grounds, trails for hill climbs, and a practice competition course.

Minnesota is in the process of allowing their statewide network of snowmobile trails to be used by other vehicles during the snowless season.

Kansas City, Missouri, in an effort to keep motorized bikes off other park lands, has set aside a marginal unproductive land area between the Missouri River and the river levee for riding the gentle hills and banked curves.

*Driving a minibike over a field in bloom to inspect the back forty*

Winston-Salem, North Carolina is building a 91.5-acre "hobby park" to accommodate so-called "nuisances," and included are go-cart and motorized cycle areas.

Oregon has legislated 1 percent of all state highway funds to be used for construction of cycle trails and footpaths—probably the first such action in the United States, and a great boon to off-roaders.

Many suburban areas, with land unsuited for housing or industry, are ideal for trails. One such area is west of Denver, Colorado where a series of hills, a meandering creek, and flat stretches of semi-arid terrain offer road experience for the beginner, and hilly and gullied land for the veteran.

Much land that is not regularly used or is abandoned offers other areas for participation. Logging roads, power lines, fire lanes, riverbanks that flood often, strip-mining pits and hills,

abandoned quarries and gravel pits can provide enjoyable riding with the motorized bike.

## YOUNG PEOPLE AND THE MINIBIKE

The young biker is faced with the dilemma of the acceptance of his hobby by some communities and the freedom and opportunity to engage in this recreational experience.

The officials of the village of Hinsdale, Illinois, alerted to the needs of minibike owners by the pleas and efforts of a 15-year-old, were convinced that the village board should set up a bike trail on a provisional basis. Representing many other boys and girls, the boy had reported that they had worked hard to earn money to buy their bikes, and wanted a safe, legal place to enjoy them. Impressed by the adult attitude and sincerity of the group, the board had approved a trail near a local lagoon. Rules were evolved

*Organized racing for youngsters develops skills for bigger machines and greater adventure.*

through the cooperation of the park board with the young people:

1. Bikes must have mufflers, governors, and pass a safety check.

2. A group of adults must supervise the trail, check for overcrowding, speeding, etc.

As a result of success in that village, others have followed suit and allow young people to use their minibikes in controlled areas, legally.

The Cook County Forest Preserve District, following the example of surrounding communities, established a minibike trail, and the district's president, George W. Dunne, met with concerned citizens to work out a plan that would eventually provide a wide system of trails in various parts of the county.

In Dade County, Florida, the Southwest Branch YMCA sponsors organized dare-deviltry rallies over a half-mile obstacle-strewn course on the wooded section of their 10-acre grounds. The races are organized in four divisions: 2½ hp and under, 3½ hp and under, 4½ hp and under, 5½ hp and under. First place winners in each division win a trophy, second and third place runners-up are awarded ribbons, and there is a best-time in the rally trophy.

All competitors must wear helmets, pass an inspection, and file a parent-consent slip. The young racers, from eight years and up, ride alone around the pine and palm-studded track, competing against the stopwatch.

To test the skill of the racers, the North Branch YMCA includes in its rally more obstacles along the hazard-strewn half-mile track. These include water holes, sandy patches, a slalom section around tires laid on the ground, a low bridge (a bar across the course under which the racers must 'duck'), hills, and a straightaway—all in close proximity.

The nature of their rallies precludes straight, speed racing. Parents and family members eagerly watch the young people compete in races that stress control of vehicle under pressure (the clock), sportsmanship, and safety.

## MINIBIKE RALLY ORGANIZATION AND SUPERVISION

The Dade County YMCA's have granted permission to reprint their Information Sheet for Contestants, a List of Officials and their Duties,

for the assistance of those interested in sponsoring minibike rallies.

## PROBLEMS CONFRONTING THE MINIBIKER

In most states, the vehicular laws consider the minibike strictly an off-road vehicle: it cannot be legally registered as a means of transportation and it cannot travel over streets or highways. Age requirements prevent the acquisition of a proper driver's license by young people.

Because most models do not have headlights or taillights, horns, and reflector buttons; have brakes, which are not all within state requirements; have small tires, which cannot handle rough road conditions; and have minimal power, which cannot keep up with the minimum speed limit and flow of traffic; the minibike belongs on prescribed trails in parks, on private acreage, or in the backyard.

Some communities and state officials claim the bikes are too small and too dangerous to license and that police forces are swamped with complaints about them and issue traffic citations to parents for allowing unlicensed youths to operate a motor vehicle.

According to some state officials, sellers of minibikes are remiss in not informing buyers of local laws and regulations governing their use. An ordinance requiring buyers to sign a statement of understanding of the law before accepting delivery of a motorbike seems to be a good start for communities that must deal with the problem in their own individual way. There are few pat answers applicable to all situations. The 2-million minibikes in use indicate a certain compatibility of the vehicle with the local citizenry: its off-road sphere of use, its excellent safety record, and supervised riding that includes the right bike, a helmet, proper clothing, and driving competence. Minibikers, as a group, cannot be swept aside by parents, city fathers, and state officials. Supervision, control, and education are the vital concerns for young people embarking on an experience in motorized riding.

## ECOLOGY EDUCATION FOR THE MINIBIKER

A sensitivity to ecology needs cannot be learned from newspaper horror stories or on a

city street corner. Experiences in the outdoors, confronting the elements, and observing first hand soil erosion, litter, hacked trees, or the absence of birds and animals, will indelibly impress upon young men and women the needs of nature, and they should seek out opportunities that will teach attitudes toward proper environment husbandry.

## The Youth Conservation Corps

Recently, the first phase of a 3-year pilot study was started by the Department of the Interior. It is operating approximately 60 YCC camps located in 36 states, the District of Columbia, and American Samoa. The program recruits young men and women, ages 15 through 18, who are selected by a local project manager.

Under provisions of Public Law 91-378, about 2,200 young people from all economic and social backgrounds were employed at YCC camps from the Everglades National Park in Florida to Mount Ranier and Olympic Parks in Washington; from Montezuma National Wildlife Refuge in New York and Brigantine National Wildlife Refuge in New Jersey to Texas, Nevada, and Utah.

The Corps members, under professional leadership, are employed on conservation projects, largely in the maintenance of Interior-managed and Forest Service-managed lands, and the building of "high hut" shelters, which are simple, rustic shelters for campers and backpacking hikers.

Most residential camps have the capacity for 50 Corps members each, although some may be as small as 11. Each member participant is paid a fixed sum for the 8-week tour of duty. After deductions, the take-home pay averages about $300 for the season.

Secretary of the Interior, Roger C. B. Morton, while visiting YCC camps in the West, stressed that, ". . . the YCC will not be a 'make-work' program. It is designed to assure buildup of environmental training for young people, gainful summer employment for the nation's youth, and performance of needed conservation work to improve the quality of public lands and water."

Experiences that offer the observations of ecology in action, and serving as a custodian of the environment, will compound the fun of off-road riding.

## Michigan's Cycle Conservation Club

An image-improving service and safety program is illustrated by Michigan's Cycle Conservation Club (CCC). The group concerns itself with trail building, safety, and community relations, and is dedicated to the idea that they can enjoy trail and minibiking without infringing on the rights of others.

The membership includes school teachers, students, working men, lawyers, medical professionals, and housewives. Many parents participate jointly with their children. Safety is a constant concern, and cooperatively, local police, the Chamber of Commerce, and driver education officials sponsor a training clinic in Lansing.

One of the CCC's main objectives is the development of trails (remote from towns) on federal and state-owned land. The present goal is to finish an 850-mile Pere Marquette Cycle Trail from Newaygo and White Cloud to the vicinity of Midland. Half of the trail is finished, cleared, and marked, and the aim is to open it up to snowmobilers in the winter.

In using the trail, each member is equipped with a Trail-Tour Route sheet that indicates exactly where to go. You can go for miles and miles without leaving the trail and being accused of cutting up the countryside. The members take pride in their well-earned image by following the rules of outdoor courtesy, in relationship to the environment, and other people as well. Observers are impressed with the fun values, camaraderie, and orderliness they see.

The present membership of 400 is dedicated to winning friends for off-road biking as an outdoor family activity. Their pattern could be followed, to good advantage, by individuals, organizations, and public agencies. For further information contact The Cycle Conservation Club, 2227 Lost Tree Way, Bloomfield Hills, Michigan, 48013.

Other organizations with extensive and vital programs where first-hand environment experiences can be gained include the local Explorer Scout unit, American Youth Hostels, Sierra and Alpine Clubs, Audubon Society, Nature Conservancy, Izaak Walton League, and other bird, hiking, and camping organizations.

*Minibiking over a snowmobile trail in Wisconsin*

# BUYER'S GUIDE

An overview of minibike companies, indicating the extent of their offerings, will help the buyer to survey the field and to make better judgements.

**Rupp Industries, Inc.** (1776 Airport Road, Mansfield, Ohio, 44903), also a snowmobile manufacturer, leads the field with a stable of 7 minibikes. At the economy end of the line, the ideal starter machine is the Rascal, a low-cost machine with its 127 cc, 2½ hp engine, single-speed clutch, 6" wheels, and rear braking system. Neophyte cyclists will welcome the Rascal (or the Bandit, a similar model) as an economical way to get started in minibiking.

The Rupp Enduro and Hustler models are designed for off-road travel; woodsbikes designed for rough duty in all kinds of terrain with their 4 hp engines. A woods-legal muffler is included, as is a kickstand for upright parking.

Price: Rascal, $139.95; Bandit, $199.95; Hustler, $269.95; and Enduro, $289.95.

**Honda, American Honda Motor Co., Inc.** (Box 50, 100 W. Alondra Blvd., Gardena, California, 90247) offers 4 mini-models below the 5½ hp class. The QA-50 is for kids or anyone in the family who is an off-road fan. The 2 speeds with an automatic clutch make mountain trails a snap to climb. Should you need to carry it across a stream, it is light enough (86 pounds) to pick up and tote.

The Motosport 350 model sports a racy tank design, low seat, kick starter, and ignition switch close to the throttle for safety. The 5-speed transmission makes it an ideal racing bike.

The Mini Trail 50 fits easily in the trunk of a car after folding down the handlebars and folding up the foot pegs. A spark-arrester muffler helps keep the wilderness just the way you found it. The soft seat can be adjusted to accommodate any member of the family.

The Mini Trail 70 represents a larger machine that delivers 5 bhp (Honda indicates their horsepower by the amount of horsepower it takes to stop the engine at 5,000 rpm) from its single-cylinder, overhead cam engine. The 4" x 10" size knobby tires roll over the roughest off-road terrain. A hand clutch and 4-speed transmission enable the driver to select his speed and power according to trail conditions.

Price: QA-50, $199; Motosport, $895; Mini Trail 50, $295; and Mini Trail 70, $265.

**Michrina Enterprises, Inc.** (630 Gibson St., Kalamazoo, Michigan, 49006) offers in their 'Lil Indian series, 8 assembled mini models and 3 in kit form.

*Rascal*

The Back-Tracker is pushed by a 5 or 7 hp Tecumseh engine, a variable ratio torque converter transmission, flotation tires, and weight of 140 pounds. There are "buddy pegs," and a seat to accommodate 2 riders, but if you wish to go it alone, use the extra space for your pack.

The Hellcat and Bearcat, both with 4 hp engines, have torque converter transmissions and weigh 100 pounds. Assembled Prices: Back-tracker 5 hp model, $374.95; Back-tracker 7 hp model, $399.95; Hellcat, $299.95; Bearcat, $269.95; Sabre, $239.95; Spitfire, $204.95; Thunderbolt, $175.95; Skyhawk, $169.95; and Cobra, $145.95.

Kit Prices: Spitfire, $184.95; Skyhawk, $145.95; and Cobra, $125.95.

Accessories: windshield, bugle horn, rearview mirror, 'Lil' Indian T-shirt, 2-speed mini-matic transmission, speedometer, and minibike carrier that bolts to the bumper of your car.

**Projects Unlimited, Inc.** (1926 E. Siebenthaler Ave, Dayton, Ohio, 45414) offers one of the smallest minibikes on the market, the Scat-Kitty, which is about knee-high. The Skat-Kitty's features include 2½ hp, 4-cycle Tecumseh engine with built-in alternator and one year manufacturer's warranty, one-piece cast aluminum frame and fenders, hi-low sealed beam lighting system, 5" wheels with low-profile Terra Tires.

Price: $297.85.

Accessories: detachable side car, seat bar, electric horn kit, canvas cover and a deck mount to lock the Skat-Kitty firmly to boats and campers.

**Yamaha International Corp.** (Box 6600, Buena Park, California, 90620) offers the Mini-Enduro which is powered by a 4.5 hp, valve-inducted, single-cylinder, 2-stroke engine. Other features include an excellent suspension system, comfortable seat, convenient controls, adjustable handlebars, and manual shifting with a 4-speed gearbox. Price: $299.

**Kawasaki Motors Corp.** (1062 McGaw Ave., Santa Ana, California, 92705) offers the Mini-Trail with a well-engineered engine of 4.7 hp that will push the bike up to 40 mph. The model folds down to fit into the average car trunk, making it ideal for camping trips. Price: $199.

**U.S. Suzuki Motor Corp.** (Santa Fe Springs, California, 90670) offers the MT-50R Trailhopper with a 3 hp engine and 3-speed automatic transmission. Other features include adjustable handlebars and seat, full suspension, and hand brakes. Price: $259.

**Indian Motorcycles, Inc.** (1535 W. Rosecrans Ave., Gardena, California, 90249) offers the Super Scrambler with 16" spoke wheels, 4.5 hp Minarelli engine, 4-speed transmission, and full circle crank. Price: $599.

**Arctic Enterprises, Inc.** (Box 635, Thief River Falls, Minnesota, 56701) offers a sleek looking mini that weighs only 90 pounds. The Whisker is powered by a Sachs 2-cycle engine with a gearbox that houses a 2-speed automatic transmission, and wide, knobby 12.5" tires that ride on 6" diameter aluminum wheels. Load-leveling rear shocks and telescopic front forks aid the driver in comfort and machine handling. For

LEFT: *Skat-Kitty*
BELOW: *Whisker*

ABOVE: *Cobra*
BELOW: *BeBe*

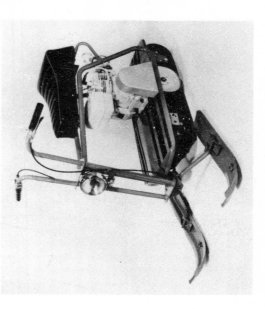

*Skee Whee*

safety, fuel shut-off valves, folding rubber foot pegs, twist-grip throttle, and shut-off switch are included.

Price: $199.95.

**Efenel Corp.** (912 W. North Ave., Chicago, Illinois, 60622) offers an array of minibikes, which carry a guarantee of 30 days on drive-train parts and 1 year on the frame.

The Cobra, their deluxe model, is constructed of 14-gauge steel tubing and has a 3½ or 4 hp Clinton engine, kick starter, buddy-type seat, gas gauge, and folding handlebars. Several suspension features insure a smooth ride over rough terrain. All Efenel bikes weigh approximately 100 pounds.

Price: Cobra, $167; Grand Prix, $119; Lightning, $99.

**Premier Motor Corp.** (Railroad Street and Plant Road, Hasbrouck Heights, New Jersey, 07604) announces a new line of BeBe mini cycles (imported from Belamotor of Florence, Italy). The BeBe includes a 5 hp, 2-cycle engine, utilizing a Dell'Orto carburetor and flywheel magneto ignition with kickstarter, swinging arm rear suspension and shock absorbers, telescopic front fork, mudguards, and 3" x 10" knobby tires.

Another BeBe model is offered with 2.8 hp engine, contour saddle seat, weight of 93 pounds, height of 22.5", and wheelbase of 37.5". BeBe Minis are available where Moto/Guzzi motorcycles are sold.

Price: BeBe, 5 hp, $299; BeBe, 2.8 hp, $260.

**F S Industries** (2021 Lee St., Evanston, Illinois, 60204) offers Skee-Whee with a unique concept in propulsion. In place of a rear wheel drive, the bike is propelled by a track system (similar to the snow-

ABOVE: *Doni*

BELOW: *Boonie Bike*

mobile) that moves the vehicle over most any terrain, light snow, sand, or grass. The moderate top speed of 25 mph, the hand brake, and the flotation tires insure safety for all members of the family in all seasons. The bike can be transported in your car trunk or station wagon.

Price: $295.

**International Marketing Associates, Corp.** (408 Lafayette Bldg., 5th & Chestnut Sts., Philadelphia, Pennsylvania, 19106) offers the Doni Minibike that folds in a minute to half its size; is fully automatic; is powered by a single cylinder, 2-stroke, air-cooled Italian Marini Giromat engine that gives out 3.9 hp; and travels 100 miles per gallon of gas. Standard equipment includes two-position headlamp, taillight, horn, tool compartment, and a 6-month warranty on all parts.

Price: $350.

*Minibike Kits*

The resourceful off-roader can save some money through the purchase of his minibike in kit form. The home-assembled product lacks none of the features contained in the factory-assembled products.

**The Heath Co.** (Benton Harbor, Michigan, 49022) offers a GT-18 "Boonie Bike" that can be assembled in one evening session. No special mechanical knowledge is required. The Briggs & Stratton engine is pre-assembled, tested, and tuned for the road, and it comes mounted on the steel frame. The entire assembly procedure is fairly simple and progresses in an orderly sequence since there are step by step instructions and giant fold-out pictorials that detail everything down to the last nut and bolt.

Once completed, you have a rugged, small, lightweight (116 pounds) vehicle with sufficient power to handle all trail conditions. An interesting accessory is the ski that can be attached to the underside of the front wheel. This functional item enables the driver to run over surf, wet sand, and snow to extend the riding season to all year round.

Price: $180.

Accessory: Ski, $20.

**Heald Inc.** (Box 1148, Benton Harbor, Michigan, 49022) offers at the top of their Trail Bronc line, the Super VT-7, a kit that includes a 7 hp Tecumseh engine, welded steel frame, padded seat, front and rear shocks, chrome-plated fenders, engine skid pan, nylon ATV-type tubeless tires mounted on 8" rims, a 1-gallon capacity gas tank, and a spark-arrester muffler.

The VT-7 will climb hills and travel on level

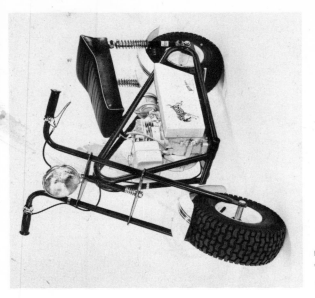

*Trail Bronc*

terrain up to 40 mph without shifting, as the throttle and brakes are the only controls. The seat is large enough for 2 adults, and there are 2 sets of foot pegs.

Price: $269.95.

Accessories: Alternator, lights, and electric start combination, $80; front ski, $19.95; tow bar, $6.95; rearview mirror, $3.95; bulb-type horn, $3.95; and tool pouch, $2.95.

Heald also offers the Trail Bronc VT-3 with a 4 hp engine. Length is 56", weight is 132 pounds, and ground clearance is 8".

Price: $209.95.

The meticulous customer in the market for a minibike may consider imports from England, Japan, Germany, Sweden, Czechoslovakia, Italy, and Canada, as well as the 50 or more United States companies, before making his choice. The buyer should make his selection on proper size and power, his experience and ability, and for the specific use to which the machine will be applied.

# 10. THE THREE-WHEEL BIKE

The three-wheel bike (trike) is an exciting new concept in go-anywhere vehicles, unique because it embodies the features of ATVs, snowmobiles, dune buggies, and trailbikes and yet is unlike any of them.

Although limited in carrying capacity, the trike is a safe vehicle because of its stability under way, and it enables the devotee to experience a wide range of terrains: the beach in front of your summer home, the trail behind a mountain cabin, the hills that are too steep to climb, and those secluded spots deep in the woods.

## DESCRIPTION OF A THREE-WHEEL BIKE

Some exceptional features of the trike make it an ideal all-family runabout.

1. Engines range from 4 hp (Bulldog) to 12 hp (Tri-Sport) with the conventional manual start.

2. Automatic transmissions control the vehicle, low gear for rough travel, and high for speeding over open country, grass, beaches, or snow.

3. The convenient controls on the handlebars regulate the speed and braking for control along the way.

4. The exhaust system is placed up and under the frame, high enough to prevent leg burns.

5. Ground clearance is adequate to keep you going even when crossing shallow streams.

6. The most identifying feature of the trike, however, is the balloon tires: two pillowy rears measuring approximately 16" x 14.5", and the narrower front measuring approximately 16" x 11.5"; all are inflated to a terrain-saving pressure of 4 psi. The bubble-ride tires offer adequate suspension, eliminating elaborate shock-proof forks and springs, yet give excellent traction in rough terrain, be it mud, sand, or snow.

7. Traction and control are enhanced by design, which places the weight of riders directly over the rear-drive wheels.

(Note: Trikes are for off-road use only; not to be used on public streets, roads, and highways.)

**Other Features** Without obstacles, some models can attain a speed of 45 mph, but most go at a more comfortable speed, and don't require the constant steering compensation inherent in many other vehicles. The trike turns on an approximate 6' radius without skidding or scuffing the terrain.

Maintenance is minimal, giving more riding time in all seasons.

For transporting your trike to the area of activity, a few twists of a wrench will break it down for hauling in the back of your car or

*Various attachments to the trike increase its utilitarian value to the suburban or rural dweller.*

station wagon. Once there, you're off—rambling, hunting, fishing, exploring, or prospecting—limited only by your imagination and judgement, or when the lady of the house says, "It's getting dark! Come in."

## UTILITY SERVICES OF THE TRIKE

Projects that require transportation through difficult terrain are suitably fulfilled by the trike: through wet fields and woods, up rocky hills, over desert sand, across shallow streams, and over snow. The trike is, in turn, a trailbike rolling over logs and fallen rocks with the balloon tires smoothing out the bumps; a dune buggy riding over undulating hills as well as through soft sand; a snowmobile twisting its way through a slalom course (in the event of an ice breakthrough on a pond or lake, the trike will float the rider); and a workhorse vehicle for many outdoor chores.

The trike is being used by fishermen for portaging an inflatable boat and tackle to back-

woods lakes, by hobbyists searching various rock formations for semi-precious gem stones, and by photographers for shooting pictures in unique scenic areas.

Various attachments to the trike increase its utilitarian value for the suburban and rural dweller. The reel-type gang mower attachment replaces the lawnmower. Professional gardeners and golf course managers recommend this type of mower because it facilitates the cutting of large swaths of grass in fairway neatness, making it ideal for the large estate, ranch, or farm. Other attachments, rented or bought, work well for aerating, rolling, and fertilizing the soil, and for hauling out trash, yard trimmings, and leaves.

## ECOLOGY AND THE THREE-WHEEL BIKE

The trike, as an off-road vehicle, is a conservationist's dream. Its limited range and speed, along with its soft squishy tires, cause little damage to the terrain and growing plant life.

## BUYER'S GUIDE

**Alsport, Inc.** (84 Whittlesey, Norwalk, Ohio, 44857) offers the TS-50, with a 5 hp standard body; the TS-100, with a 5 hp deluxe body; and the TS-150, a 12 hp model. Hardened steel axles support huge high flotation tires, 18" x 8.5" front and 11" x 21" rear, whose "gentle footsteps won't mash a marshmallow." The TS-50 weighs 140 pounds and is 81" long and 34" high. All models are maneuverable over any type of ground and on grades up to 45°.

Prices: TS-50, $445; TS-100, $495; TS-150, $565.

Accessories: roll cage (for high-speed racing), $24; seat pad, $15; windshield, $16.95; hub caps, $7.95; junior foot rest, $7.95; and 3-unit, 57" cut gang mower, $239.85.

Alsport

**Feldman Engineering & Manufacturing Co. Inc.** (633 Monroe St., Sheboygan Falls, Wisconsin, 53085) represents an example of the enterprising American, who since boyhood, toyed with the idea of a 3-wheel motorized vehicle, and in his barn workshop, after tinkering, refining, and designing, finally evolved the Mini-Brute. The trike is powered by an 8 hp Chrysler engine. An optional 11.5 hp engine is also available. All 3 tires are low pressure 11" x 20" size and exert only 2 psi. Weight is 320 pounds, length is 79", and height is 38". The welded tubular steel frame supports a neatly formed fiberglass body. The machine has a carrying capacity of 2 persons. Should extra gear or tools be needed for camping or yard chores, a tag-along trailer is available.

Price: 8 hp model, $895; 11.5 hp model, $995 (with electric start, $1,075).

Accessories: highway trailer, $185; front bumper, $18.95; hand rails, $10.95 a set; tag-along trailer, $129.50; and trailer hitch, $7.45.

**Honda** (Box 50, Gardena, California, 90247) offers an all-terrain ATC-90 trike that is powered by a 7 hp engine. The automatic 4-speed transmission, without a clutch, shifts into low for rough riding and hill climbing and into high for sand and snow traveling. When you're ready to take off, a neutral indicator lets you know that the bike is not in gear and is safe to start. Because the carburetor is adjustable, you can maintain peak engine efficiency at either high altitudes or in lowland humidity.

The spark-arrester muffler (USDA approved) keeps down the noise that reaches the ears of the driver and the environment in general.

The ATC-90 is a spunky machine that can be tricky—like flipping its pilot backward when acceleration from a standing start is too fast.

Transporting the ATC-90 to backcountry (as with all 3-wheelers) is convenient since you can pack it in your car trunk or station wagon.

Price: $495.

Accessories: lighting equipment.

*Mini-Brute*

*ATC-90*

**Sperry Rand** (Special Products Div., Lebanon, Ohio, 45036) offers the Tricart, one of the first 3-wheelers. The brightly painted monocoque, aircraft-type fiberglass body shapes the fenders and covers the chassis, engine compartment, and gas tank. The power unit is a 2-cycle JLO engine capable of delivering 11 hp and moving the machine up to 45 mph.

A Donaldson muffler provides a performance quieter than a lawn mower. The automatic transmission with Salsbury torque converter transmits power that moves the vehicle smoothly and safely, with the added feature of handlebar steering and throttling.

To activate the caliper disc brakes, push the handlebar up, which may seem unnatural, but there's a reason. When riding over bumps, the driver's natural reaction is to press down on the handlebars for support, which would cause constant and needless braking.

Stirrups for the feet, alongside the front wheel, help the driver to steer. The steering tire (front) is 16" x 11.5"; the 2 rear tires are much larger, 16" x 14.5", for better traction. This 3-wheel bike can turn within a radius of approximately 3', and the ground clearance is 9".

A newer Tricart model includes a 1-cylinder, 4-cycle Briggs & Stratton engine that generates 8 hp and gives a top speed of 22 mph, along with plenty of low-end torque, geared for pulling power. It climbs well and can be used to pull a gang mower, or it can be used as a utility vehicle to tow garden carts, haul soil, sand, bricks, etc.

Price: $715.

Accessories: luggage rack, running lights, ski rack, spark arrester, and gun rack, $359; electric start, $50.

**A.P.E. Products** (13727 Excelsior Drive, Santa Fe Springs, California, 90607) offers the Dunecycle, the least expensive and smallest of the trikes. The power plant, a 5 hp Briggs & Stratton engine, is capable of moving the vehicle at a 30 mph clip, with a climbing ability of 42°. The rear tires are oversized flotation-type, and the front minibike tire can be replaced by a snow ski. The Dunecycle is well-engineered, with a differential similar to that of automobiles, motorcycle-type twist-grip throttle, and a very long-rake chopper-like front forks. A 14 hp engine option is also available.

Price: $349 to $650.

*Arrangements for trans-porting off-road bike.*

# 11. TRANSPORTATION OF MOTORBIKES

The methods of transporting your trail, mini, or 3-wheel bike are many, and the small size and light weight of off-road cycles allow you to carry your vehicle without many problems.

The bike with collapsible handlebars and those with a hinged frame that folds in two offer the least problem. The trunk of your car, even a compact, will serve adequately.

Dismounting the rear wheel of many large bikes permits them to be slipped into the rear of a station wagon. Fasten the parts securely with tie-downs to prevent shifting.

**Types of Transportation** A bumper rack, which takes only a short time to install, can be attached to the rear bumper of a vehicle. A double rack on the rear of a trailer or pickup truck, attached to the frame, can support the weight of two bikes.

Tow bars are also used in towing the cycle to the riding area.

The conventional flat bed or box trailer, adapted with a channel rack for the front wheel and tie-downs in the front and rear, is another method. Trailers come in many styles, including some that when unhitched swing away from the back of your car, and tilt to the ground for quick and convenient loading and unloading. The conventional flat bed trailer, with proper tie-downs, will carry 2 or even 3 bikes, and serve adequately.

**Towing Tips** In trailering your cycle to rugged terrain areas, it is recommended that a strong hitch with stabilizers, firmly attached to the frame of your car, be used. Should the weight on the hitch exceed 100 pounds, heavy springs and adequate shock absorbers should be provided. The electrical system, particularly in the directional signals on the car and trailer, should be in good working condition. You should also have suitable rearview mirrors and extra air in the tires. Once underway, you'll notice that your car will accelerate a bit slower, and it will take a little longer to stop. Take it easy until you become accustomed to the added weight, as well as the distance and time required to pass and turn a corner. Know the legal maximum speeds for pulling a trailer; they differ by states.

In backing up, remember that the car's steering wheel must be turned in the opposite direction from the way you want the trailer to go. A simple trick is to place your right hand on the bottom of the steering wheel. To move the back of the trailer to the left, turn the wheel right for the opposite turn.

As an added safety measure, checks of how the cycle, or cycles, are riding should be made along the route, especially on a long trip. Not only will it give you a chance to relax from driving for a while, but it will reassure you about any worries concerning the safety of you and your trailer.

A new concept in towing cycles comes from Trail-A-Bike and includes a simple basket-type unit that attaches with 1 bolt to any trailer hitch. Two security chains are mounted to both bumper and bike, making for a rigid and secure mounting.

The bike's front wheel rests in the unit while the rear wheel runs on the ground, relieving the towing car of much load capacity, as the cycle's weight is carried by its rear wheel. The wear is due to the fact that the bike is not carrying a rider and no braking action is involved. On long trips, the rear chain should be removed from the drive sprocket for free wheeling. The chain need

not be completely removed, but rather disengaged, then wrapped in protective material and lashed to the frame.

With the Trail-A-Bike unit, towing at freeway speeds offers no problems, especially with the taillights which are included. Storage of the unit is no bother, simply hang it on a nail in your garage, leave it attached to the car, or store it in the trunk when not being used. The Trail-A-Bike unit is legal in all 50 states provided that all instructions are closely followed with regard to mounting and correct use of the supplied accessories. Sources for bike carrying attachments include:

*Trail-A-Bike, Inc.* (221 S. 19th Ave., Yakima, Washington, 98902) Model 350 for tire widths up to 3¾″, $32.95; Model 400 for tire widths up to 4″, $34.95; and DUAL (for 2 cycles), 3.5″ tread only, $64.95.

*Webco Inc.* (218 Main St., Venice, California, 90291) Universal bumper rack for most off-road bikes.

### HELMETS

In concluding the discussion on motorized off-road bikes, it is necessary to establish the importance of head protection for participants. Two-thirds of all fatalities in Illinois and Washington, according to a recent study by the National Safety Council, were caused by skull

*Trail-A-Bike units permit towing the bike at freeway speeds without problems.*

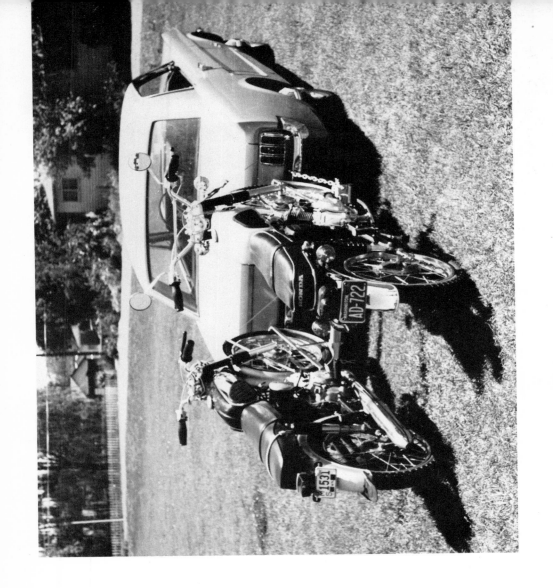

fractures. In a 6-year survey in Illinois, 2½ times more cyclists were injured or killed than were auto passengers.

Protective helmets are required by law in 42 states (as of July, 1970) according to the National Safety Council. The requirement of helmets for cyclists was tested and held constitutional by the highest courts of the following states: Louisiana, Massachusetts, North Dakota, Rhode Island, Wisconsin, and Washington. Lower courts have ruled in favor of similar laws in Connecticut and New York.

Life-saving helmets are constructed of injection-molded polycarbonate, a thermoplastic, the same as that used by astronauts and professional football players. They are lightweight and rigid

and will not crack or chip upon impact. The helmets include inner liners and chin straps, and have shock-absorbent qualities. Various designs come with shields or detachable visors, wraparound chin shields, and full face attachments with flip visors. Check the inside liner to see what tests a helmet has passed. The Z90.1-66 test standard is required by most states.

Sources for helmets include:

*Buco Helmets*, 16055 Ventura Blvd., Encino, California, 91316

*Coleman Co., Inc.*, Somerset, Pennsylvania, 15501

*General Electric Co.*, Plastics Dept., One Plastic Ave., Pittsfield, Massachusetts, 01201

*Grant Industries Inc.*, 3680 Beverly Blvd., Los Angeles, California, 90004

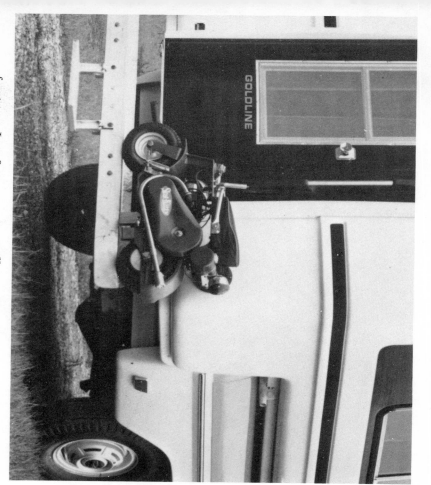

*The folded Skat-Kitty offers few problems in transportation.*

# 12. THE SNOWMOBILE

Nearly 2-million enthusiasts on the North American Continent own the leading motorized recreation vehicle—the snowmobile. The over-snow vehicle has opened to year-round use the fields, forests, and mountains, and after some 6 years its popularity threatens to pass skiing and boating—after all, the season is longer. The number of families owning 2 machines is increasing; "his" and "hers" snowmobiles are becoming more and more popular—with the youngsters borrowing either for adventures on their own. Few off-road vehicles have had such a sudden, significant, exciting, and enthusiastic impact on the American outdoor recreation scene as has the snowmobile.

Off-roaders delight in traveling along snowy trails, across many scenic portions of national forests, state and province managed lands, and private areas maintained for their use. They experience the long white views in remote places, formerly inaccessible during the snowbound season.

## THE OVER-SNOW MACHINE

Today's snowmobiles are finely engineered vehicles. The low-profile, sleek-looking machines include a 2 or 4-cycle, 10 to 50 hp engine, torque transmission, contoured hood, sealed beam headlights, dashboard, gauges, handlebar steering and controls, windshield, padded contoured seats, under-seat storage compartment, seamless gas tank, muffler, front-mounted skis, seamless moulded track, and bogie wheels.

From these basic components of the snowmobile, the companies have evolved many specialized features in their particular models, and they stand behind their products with warranties. Most snowmobile manufacturers design models yearly, and the trend is toward small, lightweight machines, a widened stance (distance between skis) for greater lateral stability, and features for more comfort and safety. The number of snowmobile manufacturers is estimated at nearly 100 in the United States and Canada, and the range of models they offer is sizeable. Complete and up-to-date information is available annually, in the early fall issues of many snow sports magazines, including: *Field and Stream*, *Outdoor Life*, *Sports Afield*, and *Invitation to Snowmobiling*.

The budding enthusiast, who is undecided about the purchase of a snowmobile should rent one, as this phase of the industry has been brisk throughout the snowbelt.

**Accessories** The range of accessories for your snowmobile runs the range from desirable, functional, additions through a welter of gimmicks and gadgets. Many of the accessories and options, depending on your personal needs, are worth the cost of immediate installation by factory mechanics. A list of the most popular accessories includes trailer, cover, electric start, tinted wind-shield, various engine modification components (for racing), speedometer, hour meter, tachom-eter, compass, temperature gauge, special ex-haust system, ski conversion (to wheels), ski shock absorbers, stable ski insert, tow bar, rear-view mirror, warm-up stand, battery charger, helmet, kidney belt, mitt grip, snowshoes, duffel and saddle bags, and rear splash shields.

**Apparel** There is probably no other recrea-tional activity that boasts the array of identifying clothes as does snowmobiling. Winter participa-tion, with the elements of snow, ice, wind

velocity, and low temperatures, obviously indi-cates a wind and waterproof insulated coverall (jump suit), thermal underwear, headpiece, goggles, mittens, and boots. The apparel offered is stylish, practical, and functional. It is loose-fitting for better insulation, has raglan or semi-raglan sleeves for better arm movement, and has heavy-duty zippers with protective flaps across the chest and legs. The jump suit can be worn over conventional warm clothing—even business suits for men, and gowns for the ladies—for that safari party at the end of the trail.

Almost every major snowmobile manufacturer offers a line of specialized clothing to make sure that participants using their machines can stay comfortable, even in the coldest weather.

Jump suits are usually big and roomy with a tough outer shell of windproof nylon, and a lin-

*Side by side bucket seating and the low-slung profile, makes the Tracker a sports car on skis.*

# YAMAHA SNOWMOBILE WARRANTY

As set forth herein, the term "machine" shall refer to snowmobile as manufactured by YAMAHA MOTOR COMPANY and sold by an authorized Yamaha dealer within the United States. Claims for warranty shall be submitted by the authorized United States dealer who performs the repairs.

**A. Period of warranty shall be:**
1. Six months from date of first use on snow.
2. Ninety days from date of first use for GP models.

**B. During the period of warranty, Yamaha guarantees to the original purchaser of each new Yamaha:**
1. Any part adjudged defective by reason of faulty workmanship or material shall be replaced free of charge.
2. Any repairs and/or adjustments made necessary by faulty workmanship or material shall be performed free of charge.

**C. To qualify for warranty, purchaser must:**
1. Complete and return warranty registration form to Yamaha within ten (10) days of purchase.
2. Submit machine to an authorized Yamaha Snowmobile Dealer for the recommended owner-responsibility service checkups outlined in the owner's manual.
3. Purchaser shall give notice to the dealer of any and all apparent defects within ten (10) days after discovery and immediately make the vehicle available for the inspection at the dealer's place of business.

**D. Warranty shall not extend to:**
1. Machines used for renting or leasing.
2. Machines used for competition racing of any kind, or machines designed specifically for racing.
3. Machines subjected to abnormal strain, neglect, abuse, or altered from standard condition.
4. Machines whose trademark, name, or identification number has been changed.
5. Machines on which parts or accessories not manufactured by Yamaha have been used.
6. Machines operated on surfaces other than snow or ice.
7. Machines repaired or adjusted by anyone other than authorized Yamaha Snowmobile Dealers, (except for normal owner maintenance,)
8. Parts replaced due to normal wear.
9. Spark plugs, clutch-drive belts, light bulbs, Batteries.
10. Machines not properly set-up by the franchised selling dealer before delivery to the retail purchaser.

YAMAHA'S LIABILITY shall be limited to that set forth in Section A and no other claims for consequential damage or injury to person or property will be admissible. All other conditions and warranties, obligations, statutory or otherwise, and whether expressed or implied, are hereby excluded.

March 1, 1971

*Your warranty is important.*

ing of synthetic pile or quilted insulation of the type used for sleeping bags. The waist is belted, and there are plenty of big pockets.

Female snowmobilers use single or 2-piece suits in chic designs: harlequin, striped, mock fur, synthetic feather, bell bottoms, Eskimo suede finish, and military uniform lines.

Sweaters of 100 percent virgin wool, turtle or mock turtleneck, and raglan sleeves are most popular as an under jump suit garment.

Jackets or windbreakers are of lightweight nylon with Dacron lining, most are water and windproof, nylon pile-lined, and have a zippered (detachable) hood.

Boots include models with imitation sealskin and rich pile lining, wool felt liners with rubber and nylon outers and drawstring tops, long furred shearling, borrego lamb, and a combination of leather and fur.

Insulated gloves (skier type) of nylon and

leather are used, as are zippered gauntlet cuff-types to keep out the snow. Mittens are preferred by many, with the addition of loose-fitting cotton or wool gloves for added warmth.

Caps should be heavy furred with earflaps or hood attachment on jacket. They not only keep the ears warm but give protection from flying snow and tree branches.

The face is particularly vulnerable to wind velocity when speeding on a snowmobile. The leather or wool masks are preferred over the plastic face shields that snap on to helmets.

For the participant's protection against glare, wind, flying snow, and branches, goggles should

*Jump suits are big and roomy, and can be worn over conventional clothes.*

be nonfogging with interchangeable lens: green for glare, amber for dull hazy conditions.

## VARIETY OF ACTIVITIES

There's a wide range of activities for the snow-mobiling participant and spectator—junior, powder puff, track, cross-country, collegiate, and high school races for the speed buffs, and for others, ice fishing, hunting, skijoring, skibobbing, cookouts, picnics, safaris, and rendezvous with members of clubs from distant locales, to name a few.

On a typical winter day, many towns blossom with "Welcome Snowmobilers!" signs on tele-phone poles, in store windows, gas stations, restaurants, and on streamers strung across "Main Street," to greet participants and specta-tors who come to enjoy some special snowmobile event. "Think Snow!" and "Stamp Out Summer" exhort bumper stickers on vehicles converging on the locale. A festival atmosphere prevails, and there are snowmobiling activities for every age and interest. There's no age, generation, or social gap, for snowmobiling is a favorite family-fun activity, club, and crowd sport.

The motorhome, travel trailer, and pickup camper, properly winterized and insulated with high capacity heater, can be set up on a camp-site and used as a base for snowmobile activities.

Information on snowmobile activities, cruising, camping, survival techniques, avalanches, wind-chill factors, apparel, and other pertinent helps are contained in *Snowmobiling: The Guide* (New York: The Macmillan Company, 1971).

**Hunting** The snowmobile enables the hunter to pursue his sport more advantageously. With the machine, he can be transported to a stand; shoot his buck, bear, grouse, or ptarmigan; and cart out the kill. The hunter can also range farther into snowbound areas where there is an early snowfall.

Some wildlife biologists, referring to the tre-mendous advantage of a motorized vehicle used in hunting, indicate that it will be necessary to reduce the big-game permits issued. When suc-cess is doubled or tripled, it follows that only ½ or ⅓ as many permits should be issued, to re-duce the overall hunting kill.

**Fishing** The snowmobile and the apparel worn help the ice fisherman to pursue his sport on lakes that formerly were inaccessible, and in

*A friendly couples' race adds a change of pace to the snowmobile outing.*

The West, particularly in the high elevations, offers spectacular snowmobile trails.

ABOVE: *The Swinger snowmobile is a light and compact machine that can easily be stood on its rear bumper for convenient storage.*

BELOW: *The Koehn Sno-Go Cab (Watertown, South Dakota) is a lightweight cover, with roll bar assembly, that fits most snowmobiles.*

temperatures that used to be discomforting. The passive nature of the sport, and the cold weather once added up to a bone-chilling experience, but with the aid of a snowmobile, the fisherman can tow an ice shanty, with a heater inside, far out to where the bluegill, perch, and walleye are biting. Tackle, equipment, and comfort-giving protection offer no burden to the machine and permit scouting a wider area of a lake.

## ORGANIZED PARTICIPATION

Snowmobiling soon nudges participants into joining with other kindred outdoorsmen in ever-widening experiences of many group activities and involvement in community projects. Snowmobile owners are a concerned lot: half of them belong to an association emphasizing their mutual interest, and in the United States, many are members of approximately 4,000 active clubs.

Those wishing to join a club may write to the secretary of their state, or province, for the names and addresses of officers of the state association of clubs, or of individual clubs within their locale (see Appendix). They will send information on dates and places of rallies, races, and special events in your area.

## TRAILS

Hundreds of miles of snowmobile trails are being added each year by national, state, and local agencies. Most are 15 to 25 miles long, and are routed over attractive terrain, beginning and ending at the same point. Increasingly, the trails are being prepared with registration stations, mileage markers, shelters, snack bars, and rest stops, enhancing the possibility of family use. Available also for the first time, in some regions, are self-guiding nature trails, and in the planning stage are ranger-guided nature rides.

Information on trails can be obtained from many sources. Federal agencies include the Bureau of Land Management, National Park Service, Bureau of Outdoor Recreation, Bureau of Sport Fisheries and Wildlife (U.S. Department of the Interior, Washington, D.C., 20240) and the Forest Service (U.S. Department of Agriculture, Washington, D.C., 20250). These agencies are concerned with serving the snowmobiler and have information on trails and maps covering vast tracts of public land under their protection.

Your state conservation department is another source of snowmobiling material: booklets giving places of participation and details on state and county opportunities, rules, regulations, registration, and fees.

Many summer wonderlands become more beautiful when the landscape is insulated with snow. Across the snowbelt, opportunity to view spectacular snowscapes is possible from the northeastern states to California.

**Eastern areas** The entire range of snowmobiling activity is available in the northeastern states on the many trails, both public and private.

Maine and Vermont snowmobilers are approaching skiers in total participation. Information, including a booklet with trail details and tips, is available from the Department of Forests and Parks, Montpelier, Vermont, 05602. The Vermont Association of Snow Travelers in Hardwick, Vermont, 05843, will also provide information.

New Hampshire locals or visitors can subscribe to *Sno Traveler*, which prints extensive coverage of snowmobile activity. Write to the New Hampshire Snowmobile Association, Box 643, Manchester, New Hampshire, 03105 for information. A White Mountain National Forest brochure, indicating snowmobiling activities, is available from the National Forest Supervisor, 719 Main St., Laconia, New Hampshire, 03246.

New York ranks high among states in total mileage of trails—many of them in the Catskill and Adirondack preserves. Old Forge, an upstate New York summer recreation area, has turned into a year-round resort area because of an excellent 500-mile snowmobile trail system. "Snowmobile Trails," with maps and information, is available from the Conservation Department, State Office Building Campus, Albany, New York, 12226.

Pennsylvania offers a leaflet describing snowmobiling and ice fishing in state parks, which is available from the Game Commission, Box 1567, Harrisburg, Pennsylvania, 17120.

**Midwestern states** Probably the greatest concentration of snowmobiles can be found in Michigan, Wisconsin, and Minnesota. A letter of inquiry to the Chamber of Commerce of any major city, or small town for that matter, will bring complete information.

Michigan offers many federal, state, and local trails. A projected plan calls for a trail from Sault Ste. Marie to Duluth across the Upper Peninsula with overnight accommodations en route. This will match the one developed by several groups that follows a horseback trail across the entire

*Snow, Skandic, and girls; what else does a man need?*

*The Continental Divide Snowmobile Trail, near Steamboat Springs, Colorado, winds through scenic vistas of mountain and meadow.*

width of the northern part of the Lower Peninsula for a distance of 251 miles. For this three day trip, riders use convenient motels at night.

In 1971, Michigan boasted over 1,000 miles of trails in national forests, 13 short trails in southern state parks, and 150 miles in northern state parks.

Wisconsin uses snowmobile registration fees to pay for a continuing program for development of trails and related facilities. From Eagle River and Rhinelander, pioneer locales of racing, to all parts of the snow-endowed state, there is a maze of criss-crossing trails: federal, state, and local. The snowmobiler who is intent on action and without reservations can merely drive along state highways and, spotting a concentration of machines, stop, unload, and get into the action.

Minnesota leads the nation with more than 100,000 registered snowmobiles—and they have the trails to accommodate them—1,771 miles

through state land; 646 miles through national forests; and hundreds of miles along abandoned logging roads, back trails, and fire lanes—totaling approximately 2,500 miles in all. Impressive, scenic, and popular runs include: Savannah, Bemidji, Paul Bunyan, Crow Wing, and Pillsbury State Forests, and Itasca State Park. Write to the Minnesota Conservation Department, 350 Centennial Office Building, St. Paul, Minnesota, 55101 for maps of state trails.

An interesting trail lies between Baudette, Minnesota and Kenora, Ontario, Canada. Along its marked course through the snow and ice islands of Lake of the Woods, it offers lunch, coffee, and rest stops. Write the Baudette Chamber of Commerce, Baudette, Minnesota, 56623.

The famous Boundary Waters Canoe Area is open for group snowmobile outings with complete outfitting—sleeping bags, tents, food, etc., and guide service—for extended trips. Write to the Ely Canoe Outfitters Association, Ely, Minne-

*The Skidozer, a track vehicle, is used to groom trails and raceways that receive heavy use.*

sota, 55731, and for the western reaches of the area, Crane Lake Commercial Club, Crane Lake, Minnesota, 55725.

**Western states** The West, particularly in the high elevations, offers spectacular snowmobiling, where the participant can ride mile after mile, day after day, without seeing evidences of civilization.

Wyoming snowmobilers boast of the Big Horn Mountains, Yellowstone, and Grand Teton National Parks, and the Wind River Range, where jutted peaks seem to nudge the sky. So vast is this country for snowmobiling that Randall A. Wagner, of the Wyoming Recreation Commission, claims, "... the thousands of parks and trails ... could easily accommodate the bulk of western snowmobilers at one time. It's a perfect spot for snowmobiling. The area is wide open, unspoiled, and uncrowded."

A popular snowmobiler mecca is the Tongue Ranger District of northern Wyoming in the Big Horn National Forest, with 5 marked scenic loop trails.

Wyoming offers trips over historic Union Pass into the headwater basin of Green River and the scenic sights of the Jim Bridger Wilderness. For points of access and other information, write the Wyoming Recreation Commission, State Office Bldg., Cheyenne, Wyoming, 82001.

Colorado has the U.S. Forest Service's recently created Continental Divide Snowmobile Trail 22 miles east of Steamboat Springs. This trail runs through a rolling patchwork of vast open areas with sheltering stands of spruce and pine. After take-off on the smooth meadows west of Rabbit

Ears Pass (elevation: 9,426 feet), the trail weaves 14 miles almost due north over varied terrain to Buffalo Pass. Three trails converge at this juncture, and choices can be made between backtracking, an easterly course to Grizzly Guard Station near Walden, or a westward course to Strawberry Park near Steamboat Springs. Scenic panoramas en route include a view of 10,719-foot Rabbit Ears Peak, the Yampa River flowing through snow-covered cattle country, and a wide valley 40 miles across at North Park.

Montana has the famous Big Sky Trail, which is unequalled, in many ways, in North American snowmobiling. From Bozeman, the trail climbs, descends, and meanders southward for 120 miles to the outskirts of West Yellowstone Village. En route the country is vast, wild, and interesting, as it sweeps through the Gallatin Valley, and farther south through countless ranges and solitary peaks jutting against the skyline. The run passes through the state-legislated elk ranges. The climax of the scenic course comes just above West Yellowstone, where the awesome Teton Range edges into view.

A practical feature of the 120-mile trail is that it can be driven in smaller segments, as 7 access points along the way enable snowmobilers to experience trail stretches of 5 to 55 miles.

Utah offers the hunter a prolific country, particularly for elk and deer near the Utah-Wyoming border south of Evanston, Wyoming, and along the Bear River toward Mirror Lake. Jack rabbits and cottontails are abundant in Duchesne and Unitah counties. For spectacular cruising, the Uinta Mountains of northeast Utah, running east and west for approximately 150 miles, contain a network of well-marked snow-mobile trails, including routes down quiet valleys carved by the many streams that tumble from the high mountains. Heavy stands of timber protect the trails from wind and drifts, and the snowpack is smooth and even.

New Mexico's most popular spot for snow-mobilers is the Cerro Valdez area in northern New Mexico; it has 30 square miles of remote rolling terrain, characterized by criss-cross trails, high hills, and snow-sculptured mesas.

Idaho's high, scenic, eastern portion offers snowmobile activities such as the interesting trek from West Yellowstone, Montana over to Mammoth Hot Springs and Old Faithful Geyser in Yellowstone Park. In Sun Valley, the snow-mobiling seems to be as popular as skiing, but

*For the speed buff, New York offers many small and big-time races.*

Snowmobilers gather in front of the snack bar during an outing in Paul-Sauvé Provincial Park in the Province of Quebec.

there's no conflict since the two groups use different terrain. For detailed information, write Idaho Fish and Game Dept., 518 First St., Boise, Idaho.

California's experienced snowmobiler, with caution, can explore California's Sierra and Cascade ranges, which rise above 6,000 feet. The areas are remote, little traveled, and are so rugged that only the experienced snowmobiler should consider the region.

## PRIVATE SNOWMOBILE TRAILS AND FACILITIES

Judging by what's happening on the hunting and fishing scene in this day of population stress and shrinking facilities, increasingly the sportsman must turn to the private shooting clubs and pay by the pound for fish caught in stocked lakes. So too, the snowmobiler in some areas must patronize a private facility.

Some include a ski-resort-type building with a main lodge, restaurant, meeting rooms, rest rooms, fuel pumps, and a heated garage for machine repair and tune-up. Guests use trails of various distance and difficulty, and along the way there are warm-up shelters and rest rooms.

Packages that include suitable trails, food, lodging not too far from home are being offered, getting takers, and filling a definite need in areas of clustered population.

The Michigan Caberfae Ski Area officials, realizing the potential for promoting their facilities for snowmobilers, do a large business in rentals. Parents of children who use ski facilities often take off in a snowmobile, and many others combine both sports on a weekend.

Hideaway Village in Winter Park, Colorado offers over 80 miles of packed and marked trails in the Arapahoe National Forest. During the day, you operate machines over the trails by yourself on snofaris, guided tours, and noon-lunch rides. At night, special moonlight group rides feature campfires and refreshments.

## ECOLOGICAL CONSIDERATIONS

Many feel that there are varied undesirable effects in the proliferation of snowmobiles— which have been around long enough to justify some solid criticism.

**Noise Pollution.** "The greatest single objection to snowmobiles is the problem of noise," reports the Environmental Quality Committee of the International Congress of Snowmobiles.

No wonder that people who are wakened at midnight by a squadron of machines or intent on a Sunday day of rest and are interrupted by noise that sounds like an artillery barrage, supremely wish for a snowless winter. Even in Anchorage, Alaska the problem is becoming acute, since there are probably more snowmobiles per capita, and per square mile, than in any other locale in the country.

There is legal recourse for harassed citizens: a nuisance complaint, for "unreasonable" and "excessive" noise is definitely considered a nuisance. There is judicial recognition of this; several state supreme courts have awarded damages for invasion of plaintiffs' property rights: noise from airplanes and autos which disturbed sleep, livestock, and, in general, made life miserable. Similarly, property owners may bring action against snowmobile users, and a court might rule that the vehicle noise is an injurious interference with a person's private use and enjoyment of land.

Noise is dispatched farther when there are no leaves on the trees to deaden the sound. In the deep wood or in the mountains, the machine sounds louder because of the quiet surroundings.

Many states, manufacturers, and club groups have concerned themselves with the snowmobile noise problem:

The California Vehicle Code sets specific decibels for all (on-road) motor vehicles, and will probably include off-road vehicles soon.

In Minnesota, Conservation Regulation 55 requires that new snowmobiles be sold with a muffler limiting engine noise to 86 decibels on the "A" scale at 50 feet.

In New York, the Adirondack Mountain Club proposed the banning of off-road vehicles producing sounds at 73 decibels on the "A" scale at 50 feet.

Michigan requires a muffler "... in good working order to prevent excessive or unusual noise and annoying smoke."

Wisconsin prohibits the operation of snowmobiles "in such a way that the exhaust of the motor makes an excessive amount of unusual noise."

Stillwater, Minnesota represents one town that has restricted snowmobile use "upon any property, public or private, lakes, and rivers between the hours of 11 P.M. and 7 A.M. of the following day."

## Other Disruptive Effects

Several cases of devegetation caused by the snowmobile have occurred, primarily to seedling trees, planting and reforestation areas, golf greens, and nurseries.

In the high elevations and northern latitudes, characterized by alpine, and arctic tundra where the growing season is short, and the root system fragile, the scarring by a snowmobile may have permanent damaging effects.

Many animals', especially deer's, forage ability is curtailed in the snowy months, and their reserve of stored energy may be marginal or critical. Being very wary, these animals will run for miles at the sound of unnatural noise and exhaustion often leads to death. This problem is ever present in the harsh winter when snowmobiles operate.

Harassment of wildlife by snowmobiles is reported: "Wildlife is frequently harassed and actually killed by snowmobilers pursuing them until they die of exhaustion," reports the South Dakota Department of Game Fish and Parks. "There is major harassment and disturbance of big game both by vehicles and aircraft in season and out," notes Manitoba's Wildlife Branch. Other complaints about snowmobilers harassing game or specifically running down deer, coyotes, fox, and other fur-bearing animals have been reported in Alberta, Saskatchewan, the Yukon, Michigan, Minnesota, and Utah.

Fish have been poached from waters previously inaccessible in the winter. To illustrate the effectiveness of the snowmobile, Pierz Lake, 16 miles off the Gunflint Trail in Minnesota can be reached in the summer only by a 6-hour canoe and portage trip, but a reporter counted 67 snowmobiles and 120 fishermen there in mid-January.

## Needs for the Future

Government agencies at many levels (state and provincial, county and municipal) and the snowmobile manufacturers believe that some steps must be taken for the good of the sport:

1. Registration of vehicles is the first step to provide identification as a basis for control.

2. Regulations and enforcement should fall under the jurisdiction of highway and conservation departments to promote uniformity of operating procedures.

3. The noise level must be controlled.

4. Respect for the property rights of private landowners and village residents must be maintained.

5. The machine should serve as an access advantage to remote places, but activities, such as hunting, should be done on foot.

6. There should be information programs to resolve some of the frictions between users of snowmobiles and non-users.

7. There should be education in proper and safe use of machines, resource conservation, and ecology through many media such as lectures (at club meetings), films, handbooks, and manufacturer's literature.

John W. Hetherington of Bombardier Ltd. adds, ". . . assure the devotion of more public and private lands to well-planned, well-controlled fun areas in which snowmobilers can safely enjoy their sport in a way which respects both other people and the environment."

The compaction charges against the snowmobile, where snow is compressed over grass, and on lake ice to prevent the sun's rays from penetrating, have not been proven as harmful effects. After all, the skier on the slopes with 6 months of compressing pressure on the snow, does not kill the grass beneath.

That the snowmobile can be a loud, law-breaking, environment-disrupting influence on the off-road scene is obvious. The undesirable effects of the snowmobile must be controlled: manufacturers must design a quieter vehicle; federal, state, and local agencies must recognize that snowmobiles are here to stay and that they must be accommodated with intelligent rules and regulations. Adequate areas of participation must be developed, and above all, the participant must accept responsibility, clean up his own house, and agree that regulations are essential to protect his values, as well as those of others.

# PART III

# Watercraft

## 13. INFLATED CRAFT

An intriguing opportunity for seeking out water frontiers is offered by the many forms of inflated craft: dinghy, raft, rowboat, canoe, yacht tender, sailboat, and motorboat. They offer adventure possibilities in out-of-the-way watery places, and still give the hard-hulled boat thrills of paddling, sailing, outboarding, and cruising. Inflated craft are ideal for fishing, hunting, snorkeling, scuba diving, salvage operations, and many other activities.

### HISTORY

Inflatable boats have a romantic history as the life-saving rafts for sailors and aviators from sunken and downed craft in peace and in war; as the craft of espionage behind enemy positions, underwater demolition, and commando raids in World War II; as life rafts for amphibious assault and staging rafts by Navy frogmen; and as the craft for shooting wild rivers and filming the oceans of the world. Jacques-Yves Cousteau uses extensively an assortment of auxiliary inflated boats in filming action shots, such as whale tagging, shark habits, etc., for his television shows, such as "The Undersea World of Jacques Cousteau," which have stimulated public understanding and appreciation of the world's oceans, their fish, and their wildlife. In NASA's space program, the Navy frogmen, in inflated boats, are on the scene immediately after splashdown to retrieve the astronauts from their capsule.

### ACCEPTANCE OF THE INFLATED BOAT

The blow-up craft is very popular in Europe, and represents approximately 65 percent of the annual total boat sales. One Parisian dealer sells an average of 250 inflatables per year.

The popularity of the inflated craft in the United States is catching on fast, and it promises to be a very significant factor in boating's future. Up to 80 inflatable boats are displayed annually at the boat shows in various large cities in the United States. Two-boat families are more and more including one inflatable in their plans. As to popularity, it is greatest in the West, then in the Midwest, and then in the East.

### THE ADVANTAGES OF AN INFLATABLE

The inflated boat has developed into a recreation craft without peer. It can be transported in its compact, deflated state by automobile, minibike, horse, or backpack, or aboard a plane or large boat. At the water's edge, the boat is unpacked and quickly pumped up into a full-blown watercraft with a foot bellows pump and a bit of foot tapping to fill the compartments with air. To do the inflation job effortlessly, an electric air

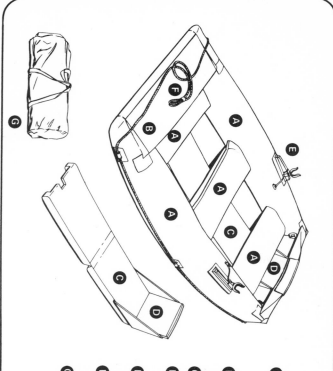

A. Five separate flotation compartments: port & starboard tubes & 3 integral thwarts.

B. Pram-type bow with marine plywood supported foredeck.

C. Removable rigid floor with twin keels.

D. Rigid transom (integral part of floor) fitted with chafe resistant motor plate

E. Delrin oarlocks mounted in teak blocks.

F. Thimbled painter bridle & all-around lifeline of 7/16″ SEA/LINE Nylon.

G. Carrying valise, heavy duty canvass Nylon stitched.

## Assembly of *Sea Boat*®

In designing SEA BOAT® we aimed at simplicity so that to assemble and make it ready for use is easily and quickly done without following complicated instructions. SEA BOAT® may be used without the floor/transom if necessary. Assembly in this case consists merely in pumping up each compartment. You cannot overinflate with the pump provided. (It will give between 2 and 3 PSI pressure normally or up to 4 PSI if forced.) A high pressure air line may be used quite safely providing you inflate only to shape and top off with the foot-pump. With practice, when you learn the "feel" of 2 PSI you may inflate to this pressure with an airline. Using the footpump for total inflation takes only 4 to 5 minutes.

*Typical assembly and folding of an inflatable*

## Fabric Construction

HYPALON (Colored)
NEOPRENE (Gray)
NYLON FABRIC
NEOPRENE (Gray)

*Fabric construction of a high-quality inflatable*

## Folding of *Sea Boat*®

● Deflate all compartments by inserting the U shaped probe attached to the valve flap into the valve.

● Remove floor/transom by sliding out sternways, and fold it.

● Roll Boat once to expel most of the air and unroll again.

● Fold sides of the boat towards middle to make width of roll 36″.

● Roll from bow towards stern, fairly tightly and push into valise.

compressor (approximately $30), which plugs into a car cigarette lighter socket, is available. In-flation of 2 to 3 pounds pressure allows the air chambers to give when hitting a sharp snag or rock and comfortable riding characteristics. A 12′ boat takes about 20 minutes to inflate, and is then ready for use. Propelled by oars, paddle, pole, sail, or outboard motor, the inflatable boat has so much buoyancy that it is practically un-tippable and unswampable. If you fill one until the water splashes over the sides, there is still plenty of freeboard and the powerhead of your outboard motor is still above water, purring and moving the craft merrily along.

Elaborate launching marinas are unnecessary,

as any shore on inland lakes, river, ocean, or other waterway suffices. Trailering is not required. The suitcase-size of a deflated boat is a fine advantage for storage and transportation where apartments and cars are necessarily compact. Storage between periods of use is in a closet or garage corner. An inflatable with a motor suitable for water skiing can be left permanently in the trunk of even a compact car, saving the cost of a trailer along with all the miscellaneous problems of licensing, insuring, hitching, and wiring.

As inflatables come of age, the choice of models broadens. The price range runs from the 1-man inflatable rubberized boat ($24.50) through the Albo-275 ($300), which is capable of taking a 5 hp motor and towing a skier and up to the 12-man inflatable ($2,000), that has crossed the Atlantic Ocean.

## TYPES OF INFLATABLES

The type of fabric used and the quality of construction separate inflatable boats into clearcut categories:

1. The plastic beach inflatables are usually made of vinyl plastic fabric that is easily punctured, and seldom give more than 1 season's use. They should not be considered seriously if you are interested in either safety or extensive use of an inflated product.

2. The next group consists of life rafts for emergency use in large boats and airplanes. These rafts come with $CO_2$ containers for quick inflation. Many have a canopy over them and emergency supplies stowed in the bow. Lightly made for short time use, they will not resist the abrasion of normal boat handling. Once inflated, emergency rafts require a return to the factory or service station shortly thereafter to be blown clean, because the $CO_2$ creates a chemical action which causes deterioration to the neoprene. The boats are reusable, but only after servicing.

3. Of most interest to the off-road outdoorsman is the inflatable of higher quality, constructed of neoprene-treated nylon fabrics. The nylon fabric gives the boat its strength, and the neoprene provides watertight seal. Craft with this construction are virtually puncture-proof, and last from 10 to 15 years. Guarantees by manufacturers generally run up to 5 years. Air valves are important. They should be of a large bore to quickly pass air for inflation and defla-

tion, corrosion-proof and fool-proof in conditions of sand and saltwater. Screw-fitted valves of plastic or brass, along with a pressure gauge, are preferable and are included in more expensive models.

These boats fill the needs of rugged cruising for varied outdoor purposes, and are generally designed for use with outboard motors. As many are used in heavy-duty boat service as are enjoyed in pleasure activities. According to Robert L. Cox of Lauderdale Marina, one model is hefty enough to be used with twin 40 hp outboard motors. That the inflatable boat is serviceable, durable and safe, is attested to by the organizations that use them: the United States Navy and Marine Corps; the French, Italian, and Israeli Navies; the Portuguese Army and Navy; and various police, fire, and customs departments.

Zodiac Company research has evolved many sound principles for inflatable boats:

1. If a boat is too narrow, its stability suffers.
2. If a boat is too large, it is too slow.
3. If the air chambers are too large in diameter, little inside space is left for passengers.
4. If the air chambers are too small in diameter, the passengers will get wet, and stability and load-carrying capacity are diminished.

The inflatable is not a cheap version of conventional boats. The smaller models (8' to 15') generally cost as much, or more, than a boat of the same dimension in fiberglass or wood. In larger sizes, inflatables can be bought for less than their counterparts in fiberglass or wood.

## VARIOUS DESIGNS OF INFLATED CRAFT

Manufacturers have designed and tailored inflated craft to approximate the contours and functions of a canoe, sailboat, and motorboat.

### The Inflated Canoe/Kayak

Because of the similarity of a canoe and kayak, they are discussed as a single craft. Their counterparts in rubber cannot capture the nuances of design adequately to differentiate them: however, none of the advantages of a canoe—streamline design, ease of propulsion, or lightness characteristics—are sacrificed in its inflated version.

The mini-size canoe fits into the rear of a station wagon without deflation and offers an ideal craft for cruising and fishing, transporting and portaging. It is a natural for use on farm ponds and nominal-sized lakes and streams. Types of propulsion are varied and paddle, double-bladed oars, pole, or sculling paddle may be used for quiet progress, whether for stalking a wily bass or an easily-spooked waterfowl. Many water recreationists have switched to inflatables.

(Note: The folding boats with a solid wood or metal skeleton covered by various types of tough and resilient skins have a long history—over 80 years—of serving explorers, geologists, hunters, fishermen, and whitewater fans. They will not be discussed here.)

## The Inflated Sailboat

The inflatable craft rigged with a sail brings the sport of sailing inexpensively to thousands; it is an ideal first sailboat for introducing children to the sport. Its soft approach will do no harm and can help novices to avoid making enemies of nearby boat owners. Most will point up nicely to the wind, and come about without hesitation. The mast stepping unit installs without screws or bolts, and the synthetic sails and aluminum masts require little maintenance. The rudder, pintle assembly, and tiller are usually one unit that clamps onto the transom in a matter of minutes. The entire rudder assembly usually flips upward,

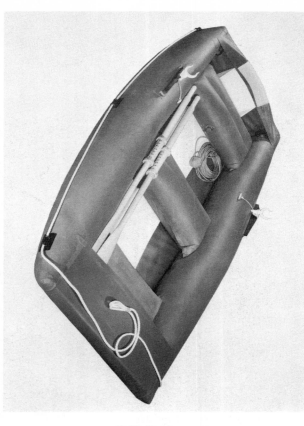

*The fully-inflated boat has so much buoyancy that it is practically untippable and unswampable*

allowing the craft to be launched off a shallow beach.

## The Inflated Motorboat

The constant vibration of an outboard motor secured to a small boat is worrisome, the transom may work loose, dropping motor and stern into the drink and creating an embarrassing problem. With the construction of inflated sides, wooden transoms, and floorboards that absorb the shimmy effect of motors, the inflated boat adequately absorbs the motor's vibration. The low draft feature of the inflatable, drawing little water, enables the motor power to effortlessly zoom it along.

Generally, motorized inflatables can do anything a hard-hulled boat can do, and possibly better. They draw less water, turn sharply, and have much faster initial pickup. Their light weight gives better economy in gas consumption. Some models have an inflatable keel to help steering since there is not much boat below the water surface.

## THE VERSATILITY OF INFLATED CRAFT

The inflated craft is practically maintenance free—no painting of rusted areas; no pampering

ABOVE: *Motorized inflatables can do anything a hard-hulled boat can. This one, with a 115 hp motor, accommodates a family of 6 in comfort.*

BELOW: *Teamed up with the airplane, the inflatable boat travels as a piece of luggage, then at the chosen site, it is inflated and launched.*

*Driving a 15' Zodiac, Ed Joyce completes a 58 mile run from Ft. Lauderdale, Florida to Bimini.*

or replacement of parts. Afloat, it has the tremendous advantage of flexibility: it flexes in tight quarters and negotiates reefs, sand bars, jagged rocks, and other underwater hazards that would tear out the bottom of a wood or metal boat. As to weight comparisons, the inflatable boat has only ¼ of the weight of a comparable aluminum boat. That the 4-man inflatable, carrying a half-ton of cargo will not sink, even when completely swamped, demonstrates its safety margin. The newer inflatables are compartmentalized, so that punctures affect only a part of the craft, and it remains afloat, disproving a general conception that an inflated boat, when punctured, will pop like a balloon. Tears and punctures under water tend to minimize escaping air because of the low pressure in the chambers, which are independent of one another.

The inflated boat does not ride high enough out of the water to be a big wind hazard, and along with the built-in seats, the high cushiony sides are comfortable for sitting. Enhancing stability at full speed is the V-shaped hull that enables the boat to climb the waves. The transom is placed slightly rearward of the stern to further enhance stability in rough water.

The characteristics of an inflatable make it a bit difficult to row, especially without the inflated V bottom. Because the lack of glide after an oar stroke, short quick strokes are recommended.

## Varied Uses

1. The small inflatables are not new to the seagoing yachtsman, who is accustomed to carrying a small boat (tender) piggyback aboard his larger craft. They are self-fendering, and prevent damage to the parent ship. They tow well and do not require expensive davit installations; neither do they contribute to the weight and windage disadvantages on the cabin top. Most small cruisers can accommodate only an eight-foot dinghy of the rigid boat type that are good for up to 3 hp motors, slow and relatively unstable. This same cruiser, using an inflatable, can have a larger, very stable tender, which can take much more power, and can serve as a substantial lifeboat.

2. For the camper who wishes to take a boat along, regardless of the road vehicle he uses, the inflatable is the ideal answer. Instead of transporting a rigid boat on the roof of a car or truck, adding to height and windage, or on a trailer with all its attendant problems, the camper can have a stable boat which does not require cartopping, trailering, or a launching ramp. The inflatable can be hand carried to any likely looking water for nautical or subaquatical sports, or river fishing, duck hunting, etc.

3. Teamed up with the airplane, the inflatable boat travels as a piece of luggage, then at the chosen site—a wilderness lake or local storm-tossed water where help is needed—the boat is unpacked, inflated, and launched. As a rescue boat, the inflatable can come alongside a vessel in heavy waters that would smash a small, rigid boat. Inflatables are standard craft for many rescue squads.

## SOME FEATS PERFORMED BY MEN IN INFLATED BOATS

A group of 9 navigators (5 Spanish and 4 French) under the command of José M. Maso, crossed the Mediterranean Sea from Palma de Mallorca to Barcelona, Spain, with three Zodiacs powered by 40 hp Evinrude motors. The crossing was a first, for the 135 miles were clocked at 10½ hours.

A Yugoslavian doctor, Mikenko Popovic, circumnavigated the Balkan Peninsula in the Adriatic Sea.

Alain Bombard, after conquering the English Channel and the Mediterranean in a Zodiac Mark III, spanned the foreboding waters of the Atlantic Ocean to reach the West Indies.

The unique feat of powering a "rubber" boat from Fort Lauderdale, Florida to Bimini, a distance of 47½ miles, in 2 hours and 38 minutes, by Ed Joyce, was intended to call attention to the utility and performance of the inflated hull. The 14-foot Zodiac inflatable was powered by a 40 hp Johnson to an 18-knot average over the distance.

Sergio Croci, with 2 companions, used a 22-foot rubber dinghy to cross the Pacific Ocean from Peru to Polynesia, a distance of 4,119 miles, in 70 days.

## CARE AND MAINTENANCE

Although most inflatables are resistant to the effects of oil, grease, saltwater, and sunlight, and include many more advantages, some care and attention is required for a long life and trouble-free cruising:

# Suggestions For Use

Rowing. Use good, strong 6' oars (Cat. #52-412 or equivalent) not flimsy paddles. SEA BOAT® is designed to be rowed like a conventional dinghy.

Loading. Load evenly so that a near level or slightly bow up trim is maintained where possible.

Outboard Motor. Transom height is 14½'' which is the correct height for any standard shaft outboard motor. You would normally need 1½ to 3 H.P. but the transom is stressed to take up to 10 H.P. Do not leave an outboard motor on the transom when boat is moored unattended.

Towing. SEA BOAT® will tow more easily than any rigid dinghy because of its light weight and resilience. It will not damage the towing yachts counter when it overtakes in following sea conditions. Best way to tow is by using the bridle painter attachment with SEA BOAT® hard up to counter.

Carrying on Deck. Some owners like to carry an inflatable dinghy on deck partly inflated to save space while it doubles as an emergency dinghy. SEA BOAT® can be stowed this way partly deflated in a variety of ways:

- Deflate thwarts. Space occupied 8'-2'' x 2'-0'' x 1'-2''.

- Deflate center thwart and soften side tubes until bow folds over to stern. Space occupied 4'2'' x 4'0'' x 2'0''.

- Deflate side tubes, remove floor/transom which would not be needed for emergency dinghy role. Space occupied is size of three thwarts, ie. 4'6'' x 3'0'' x 1'0''.

Recovering exhausted swimmer or heavy salvage. SEA BOAT® has the unique advantage that the bow section can be used like a whale factory ship in miniature. By removing the plywood foredeck, deflating the bow thwart and softening the centre thwart, the boat is still seaworthy but will allow a heavy object or exhausted swimmer to be dragged aboard at the bow, virtually at water level without lifting. Once aboard the thwarts can be reinflated if desired and the boat baled or pumped dry.

LEFT: *Suggestions for the use of the inflatable*

BELOW: *Repair procedure*

# Repair Procedure

- Clean damaged area with abrasive and finish with rag dampened with gasoline.

- Cut a patch 1'' larger than the damaged area and clean face.

- Apply three coats of adhesive to patch and to damaged area allowing first coat to dry and second to be tack dry. (Do not let dry.)

- Apply tacky-dry patch taking care not to trap air bubbles. Press firmly into position and with a roller (or a cylindrical object like a screwdriver handle) continue to apply pressure with a rolling action.

**NOTE:** If the damage has penetrated the fabric and the neoprene coating, it is necessary to impregnate the area well into the edges of the fabric around the damage.

1. Inflate your boat to the pressure indicated by the manufacturer.

2. Never use a high-output (gas-station) air hose for inflation.

3. Never step on an inflated boat when it is resting on the ground.

4. Overloading and overpowering, as in all watercraft, should be avoided.

5. Stability, the center of buoyancy, is adversely affected by standing in a boat.

6. Kneel on the seat or remain seated when landing a fish or adjusting, refueling, or starting an outboard motor.

7. On river travel, plan to go ashore when the legs feel cramped.

8. Wash boat with fresh water after extensive use. Clean the inside of the boat of debris and sand, stones, twigs, or other hard objects since they tend to work below the floor and corners to eventually cause chafe.

9. Boats with rigid insets, floorboards, etc., should be checked periodically for chafing or wear at junctures.

10. After cleanout and wash, allow the fabric to dry and then stow the boat (inflated) under shaded cover (not in direct contact with radiators, heaters, or hot pipes).

11. Periodically paint floor/transom unit with marine paint or varnish. Areas of wear are best painted with an aerosol spray.

## THE ADVANTAGES OF INFLATABLES

The inflatable craft fills a definite need for many people:

1. People who vacation in travel trailers, and cannot pull a high-performance boat behind them.

2. People who object to the reduced speed limit imposed on a car or truck pulling a boat on a trailer.

3. People with storage problems who don't have room to park a trailered craft.

4. Adventuring people who may wish to explore water frontiers and know that suitable launching places are few.

## BUYER'S GUIDE

Your local marine dealer is probably stocking a line of inflatables. Most of those sold in the United States today are imports from England, France, Italy, and Japan, which leads in the production in play models. But, American manufacturers are rapidly closing the gap in all types of inflatables.

Standard and optional equipment vary with the different companies, and the buyer should ascertain whether the following are included or optional: oars, floorboards, windshield, spray shield, ditty bag, transom, and, when to be used with an outboard, motor mounts and steering mechanism.

Again, as in all previous quotations, the following prices are approximate, and subject to change without notice.

**James Bliss and Co., Inc.** (Dedham, Massachusetts, 02026) offers a 1-man inflatable rubberized boat. The inflated size is 4'2" x 72".
Price: $24.50.

The 2-man boat may be used as a dinghy or for river touring, hunting, or fishing. The inflated size is 94" x 54".
Price: $52.50.

The 4-man size, rigidly tested for safe outdoor sports on water, is constructed of heavy-duty multi-ply rubberized canvas cloth, and inflates to 112" x 58".
Price: $75.00.
Accessory: aluminum oars, $7.50 per pair.

The 7-foot boat may be used as an emergency life raft or as a cruising yacht's tender. Its sharply upturned bow and nylon bow weather shield provide a neat storage locker to keep gear dry in bad weather. Total buoyancy evenly loaded is 1,200 pounds. It comes complete with oars and repair kit.
Price: $325.00.

The C Craft Dinghy, 8 feet in length, may be rowed, or with the optional motor bracket, a 3 hp motor will propel the boat with a capacity of up to 4 persons. There are no metal parts to corrode and there is little maintenance.

Accessories: outboard motor bracket, $27.50; extra repair kit, $2.50.
Price: $335.00.

The largest boat in the line, C Craft Outboard Boat, has an overall length of 9'3", weight of 89 pounds, swamped buoyancy of 1,090 pounds, a carrying capacity of up to 5 persons, and an outboard motor capacity of up to 10 hp. Standard equipment includes floorboards, battens, transom, wooden seat, oarlocks, sculling oarlock, foot pump, jointed oars, fitted spray shield, repair kit and instruction book—all packed in 3 individual canvas carrying bags.
Price: $565.00.

**Leisure Imports, Inc.** (104 Arlington Ave., St. James, New York, 11780) has received many testimonial letters from users of their boats in the Rocky

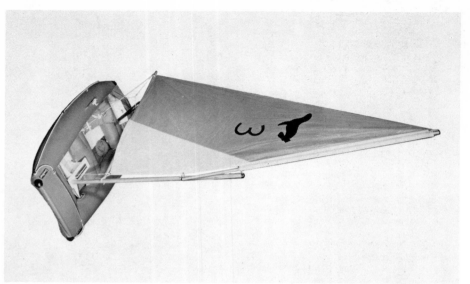

*The Sailer transforms easily from a pram dingy into a sailboat.*

Mountains, British Columbia, Oregon, Texas, and many other places.

Their P-3 model has a load capacity of up to 3 people and 800 pounds. Its dimensions of 9'5" x 4'3½" give best performance with a 6 hp motor, but up to 10 hp may be used. The inflatable keel, between the bottom of the boat and the removable floor, assures better control and improves planing and speed.

Price: $389.95.

The P-4 model carries up to 4 people for water sports at sea or on lakes. Best performance is with 10 hp motor, but 20 hp is needed for water skiing. Dimensions are 10'10" x 4'11".

Price: $379.95.

Accessory: Over-all cover, $27.99.

**West Products Corp.** (P.O. Box 707, Newark, New Jersey, 07101) claims that their Sea Boat is the best inflatable dinghy available. This entry in the inflatable field is not an import and since West

has only the 1 model, it is able to concentrate more on design and construction. The Sea Boat is designed like a pram dinghy, which holds spray down to a minimum and gives the advantage of providing extra storage space, allowing oars to be carried inboard. The exclusive design involves a 1-piece floorboard and transom unit, which eliminates bolts and nuts, sliding fittings, locking devices, and fastenings. The Sea Boat measures 8'2" x 4'2"; weighs 70 pounds; and has a capacity of up to 5 persons, a total buoyancy of 2,200 pounds (dry) and 1,200 pounds (swamped) and a motor capacity of up to 10 hp. Standard color is grey, with blue, yellow, and white as options ($10 extra). The double coating of neoprene and hypalon-coated nylon exceeds the military specifications for the U.S. Navy inflatable boats.

Price: $279.00, complete with valise, inflating pump, oarlocks, and repair kit.

Accessories: Floor/transom, floordeck, and motor plate, $73; 6' hardwood oars, leathered and buttoned, $19.95; extra foot pump, $5.95.

A sailing kit transforms the Sea Boat into the "Sailer" model, which lends itself to good performance under sail. The rudder, pintle assembly, and tiller are one unit that clamps onto the transom in seconds. The hinge on the rudder allows the Sailer to be launched from, or sailed onto, a beach.

Price: $288.00, complete with valise, dagger board sleeve, straps, pump, oarlocks, and repair kit.

Accessories: Floor/transom, foredeck and transom plate (sailing version), $77; 2'6" paddle, varnished, $3; sailing gear; spars, mast step, dagger board, lifting rudder, rigging sail and sailbag, $180.

**Zodiac of North America, Inc.** (subsidiary of Zodiac, France, 11 Lee St, Annapolis, Maryland, 21401) manufactured dirigibles as early as 1908. Later, it entered into inflated boat production for the military, and today, it is completely involved in the sport of boating with a full line of boats.

The Dinghy, which measures 9'2" x 4'7", is approved for use as a life raft. Its weight is 44 pounds. It has a load capacity of 900 pounds, and can accommodate a motor up to 4 hp. Two buoyancy chambers with a single inflation point, rear oarlock, and oars are included. This model is approved for pleasure craft, in France, within offshore limits of 200 miles.

Price: $441.00.

The Junior, which measures 10'6" x 4'10" and weighs 106 pounds, has a load capacity of 900 pounds. This model takes an outboard of up to 25 hp and includes 2 buoyancy chambers, inflatable keel, floorboards, stringers, and oars.

Price: $622.00.

The Mark I measures 10'6" x 4'10", weighs 111

*Scuba diving in a sheltered cove off the coast of France from a Zodiac is the "good life" personified.*

pounds, and has a load capacity of 900 pounds. A deck provides a spacious area for storage. It takes a motor of up to 25 hp, and includes 2 buoyancy chambers, inflatable keel, floorboards, stringers, self bailers, pressure gauge, and oars.

Price: $638.00.

The Mark II (compact) measures 12' x 5'6", weighs 120 pounds, and is capable of carrying 1,120 pounds. This model attains a speed 22 mph with a 15 hp motor and can take a motor of up to 33 hp. Features are the same as above.

Price: $757.00.

The Mark III measures 15'5" x 6'3", weighs 210 pounds, and has a load capacity of 2,200 pounds. This model can take a motor of up to 60 hp, and includes 5 air chambers, 4 side carrying handles, splash guards, and all the features of the above models.

Price: $1,144.00.

Mark V measures 19' x 7'10", weighs 418 pounds, and has a load capacity of 3,300 pounds. It takes a motor of up to 90 hp and is rugged enough to support 12 divers with gear. Includes 5 separate air chambers, inflatable keel, foredeck, towing rings, six side handles, floorboards, 2 stringers, self bailers, transom for twin engines, pressure gauge, and oars. Standard equipment on all Zodiac models includes carrying bags, bellows, mooring line, and repair kit.

Price: $2,075.00.

Accessories: sea anchor, $7; towing rings, $17;

oars, pair, $17; pressure gauge, $10; outboard engine bracket, $21; and many others.

**Recreonics** (29 Mileed Way, Avenel, New Jersey, 07001) offers various models.

Eagle Sailboat measures 12'6" x 5'5" and has 85 square feet of nylon sail, jointed mast (for easier transportation), transom, floorboards and centerboard, 2 air chambers, Boston valves, 3 carrying bags, and repair kit.

Price: $1,800.00.

Speedyak-100 measures 12' x 6', carries 6 passengers, and takes up to a 35 hp outboard. Features include a windshield, spray cover, plywood floor, keel, transom, 2 air chambers, Boston valves, self-locking oarlock, rubber carrying handles, hand lines, rear bumpers, drain plug, carrying bags, and tow rope eyes for pulling 1 or 2 skiers.

Price: $840.00.

Other models include: Speedyak-75, $600; Speedyak-60, $480; Bermuda, $360; Surf-rider, $240; and 3 small caravelles: K63, $72; K53, $48; and K33, $30.

**Nemrod Metzeler** (S.A. Barcelona, Spain, through its United States outlet, Hispania Motors, Inc., 11 Stone St., New York, New York, 10004) also offers various models.

All Nemrod Metzeler boats are constructed in solid colors with 3 layers of hypalon-nylon-neoprene skin and are resistant to the effects of oil, grease, seawater, light, and ozone. The flooring is made of finest quality marine plywood and is protected by several coats of water-repelling varnish. Each boat is delivered with the following items: demountable floor, pair of oars, support for prow round-house, keel, rubber foot-pump, repair kit, and canvas carrying bag.

Tender-275, a 9-foot craft capable of supporting a motor of up to 4 hp, can carry 2 to 3 people. Its total weight is 43 pounds.

Price: $285.00.

The Alba-275, also a 9-foot craft, has an engine capacity of up to 5 hp and a 2 to 3 person capacity. Weight is 60 pounds.

Price: $300.00.

The Alboran-330, top of the line, has a 10'10"

*The Alboran-330 powered by a 10 hp motor propels the boater at a 19 mph clip*

length with an engine capacity of 10 hp that propels the craft at 19 mph. Weight is 80 pounds.

Price: $350.00.

**Kayak Corporation of America, Inc.** (7 East 38th St., New York, New York, 10016) is an importer and distributor of several lines of inflatable boats including Aigle Hutchinson's and Nautisport's.

Atlanta (from Aigle Hutchinson) measures 9' x 4'2", weighs 55 pounds, has a capacity of 750 pounds, accommodates motors of up to 6 hp. The yellow-colored boat has an encased transom and wooden floor with 4 sections that are anchored by 2 side battens. Standard equipment includes a carrying bag, foot pump, repair kit, wood floor, built-in spray guard, two rear bumpers, keel strips, and oarlocks.

Price: $250.00.

Accessories: sectional oars, $15; inflatable seat, $20.

Armor 40 (also from Aigle Hutchinson) measures 12'4" x 5'3", weighs 176 pounds, has a load capacity of 1,320 pounds, and accommodates motors of up to 40 hp. The grey-colored boat, deep, roomy, and safe, is ideal for water skiing, fishing, and rescue missions. Although much larger, construction features are similar to the Atlanta. Standard equipment is the same as for the Atlanta model.

Price: $750.00.

Accessories: sectional oars, $20; inflatable seat, $25; deluxe steering assembly, $150.

Speedyak 300 (from Nautisport) measures 9'2" x 48"; weighs 50 pounds; is a sturdy versatile boat for fishermen, duck hunters, and skin divers; and can

double as a dinghy for cabin cruisers and yachts. The boat is constructed of a structural tri-laminate surface of neoprene and hypalon that is fused into nylon for maximum shock resistance and has hot vulcanized air chambers. The model takes motors of up to 6 hp and is capable of attaining speeds of up to 15 mph. Standard equipment includes reinforced carrying bag, two rear bumpers, keel, and oarlocks.

Price: $250.00.

Accessories: sectional oars, $15; inflatable seat, $20.

Speedyak 330 (also from Nautisport) measures 10' x 4'4", weighs 77 pounds, and can take a payload of up to 5 persons or 950 pounds. Inflation is through two patented heavy-duty Boston valves. The wooden floor is secured to the transom with metal struts. The wooden keel and the bottom, which are reinforced with rubber strips, insure maneuverability. Motor capacity is up to 15 hp. Skin construction and standard equipment are the same as in the Speedyak 300, except that two carrying bags are included.

Price: $350.00.

**Sears** (Department 606, Chicago, Illinois, 60607) offers 4 inflatables ranging from the 2-man craft, to a 4-man inflatable that is capable of supporting a small outboard. Oars, patching kit, and hand pump are included.

Price: $46.00 to $130.00.

*Ecology*

Beyond all of the other advantages indicated for the inflated craft, it draws few complaints from environmentalists and conservationists.

*Canyonlands Expeditions boat entering the final part of Big Drop Rapid in Cataract Canyon*

# 14. INFLATED CRAFT
# FOR WILD RIVERS

The inflated craft really comes in for fantastic adventure when it is used for the wilderness-floating, body-jostling, breath-taking expedition down such wild rivers as the Colorado, Stanislaus, Salmon (the River of No Return), Yampa, and Rogue, to name a few. These rivers have many stretches of calm water, but then in the confinement of rocky walls (up to a mile high), fallen trees, and obstructing boulders, they scream, bellow, and roar in protest, while you ride their backs in a feather quilt-type of raft.

The rafting rivers are of a special character—a million years in the making. Situated mostly in the Rocky Mountains, they flowed before birds and mammals appeared on earth and today give the off-roader a dramatic insight into geological time and his place in it. The eternal flow of water, slicing its way through solid rock to carve out Grand Canyon-size gorges, then meeting restricting granite in its path and bursting upward so that you can't distinguish where the water ends and the sky begins, is an ageless drama for all to enjoy—from the lap and bosom of a mothering craft—large, buoyant, secure, and safe.

## THE WILD RIVERS

Consider the Colorado for openers: 60,000 cubic feet of water per second struggling to funnel through a right angle turn in a narrow chasm, while a huge monolith blocks its path; a 3,200-foot drop in 300 miles that makes for a lot of disgruntled water and discordant music; the bow of a 33-foot raft hitting the turbulence, its bow virtually pointing to the sky; and whirl-pools of water sucking down the debris to Davy Jones's Locker, or whatever is its counterpart in wild rivers.

However all is not frenzy on the Colorado, for as it weaves through Canyon Lands National Park, there is a calm stretch of water with exciting views of canyons and caves, arches and minarets, and stone sentinels and flying buttresses, the spectacular artwork of the elements and of erosion over millions of years.

California's Stanislaus River, in Sierra gold rush country, presents an ideal introduction to whitewater adventure for people who have never before rafted a wild river.

Tuolumne River, in California's Wild River Parkland, offers a 17-mile raft adventure with Sutherland's Chute, where the river narrows to a 30-foot passage full of froth and frolic; pristine wilderness and abundant wildlife; meadows of wildflowers; and steep rock canyons.

American River (South Fork) is a dazzling Sierra river with dancing rapids and quiet riffles that take the floater to Coloma, where gold was first discovered in California.

Klamath River, in California, is more than a

*The Middle Fork of the Salmon Rivers offers adventure at every bend, as it races through Idaho's Primitive Area. (An ARTA sponsored trip)*

river: it is a mountain range, a marsh, a tribe of Indians, and a crossroad in the exploration and settlement of the early West. As a river, it's exciting course includes such rapids as Hamburg Falls, Rattlesnake, and dozens of others.

Cooper River, in Alaska, drifts past the peaks and glaciers of the Chugach Mountain Range, as seals, following the spawning salmon upstream, poke their heads out of the water to enliven a rafter's trip. The grizzly bear can be seen along the shore, and the bald eagle, trumpeter swan, ducks, and geese fly overhead.

In Big Bend National Park, Texas, the Rio Grande River flows through canyon walls 1,500 feet high, then within lower banks, affording a dramatic introduction to the desert land of striking contrasts in flora and fauna.

The Yampa and Green Rivers are the canyon rivers of Dinosaur National Monument, Utah. They provide access to the Age of Dinosaurs, entombed in subterranean swamplands that have turned to rock and been buried by the debris of infinite time.

Oregon's Rogue River is considered an ideal rafting river for families—easy access, excellent swimming, passage to side canyons and mountain trails, ever-changing wilderness, broad grassy meadows, feeder streams, and waterfalls.

The middle fork of the Salmon River offers adventure at every bend, as it races through Idaho's Primitive Area, a rugged land of mountains, pine forests, and wildlife and the final retreat of the Indian.

The Snake River, near Jackson Hole, Wyoming, offers unequaled views of the Grand Tetons and Jackson Hole grandeur, a fishing river supreme. Youghiogheny River in western Pennsylvania represents probably the only eastern wild river that offers rafting possibilities for one-day trips.

These rivers remain wild and remote, clean and free—mainly because of their inaccessibility, away from littering homo sapiens, and debauching industrial complexes. A note of concern must be mentioned. Many sections of the rivers are earmarked for inundation by dams—forever silencing their feral songs. Lou Elliot, Director

*ARTA offers a Paddle Option, in which participants paddle much of the numerous wilderness rivers in the West*

of The American River Touring Association, says it best: "We invite you to join us on these rivers to discover the wild beauty that will be lost to us and our children if the dam proposals succeed. We invite you to feel the joy of rapid spray, to float serenely with quiet current, to explore solitary side-canyons and the relics of Indian and early Gold Rush times. We invite you to flow with the natural rhythms of wildness."

### THE INFLATED RAFT

It's not a conventional raft you'll take down a rock-strewn river with high cliff shorelines, along snaky courses and switchbacks, but rather a hardy expression of inflated craft. They run the range from the 7-foot solo job, to the 37-footer with broad beams and 12 air chambers. The army assault craft, the surplus inflatable pontoons like those the military uses to span rivers and modern creations represent inflatable craft that are virtually unsinkable. Outboard motors are sometimes used in addition to the manual oars to control the rafts. Lifelines strung around the perimeter of rafts offer ready handholds. When the smaller rafts are used, 2 or 3 are often tied together to increase their security; all are big, bouncy, fool-proof, and safer than an automobile.

### THE INFLATED CANOE

The inflated canoe, pointed at both ends and propelled by a double-bladed oar, is the ultimate in shooting whitewater, where control and responsiveness of craft are required. It has brought safety to the fast growing sport of running the singing waters. Many whitewater clubs, realizing that, with one slight miscalculation, a raging current in rock-strewn waters can destroy a canoe in seconds, have turned to inflatables with their multiple, separately inflated air compartments, which make destruction virtually impossible. Furthermore, the craft retains the maneuverability of a canoe, while gaining the safety and comfort features of an inflatable.

The inflated canoe, besides being an ideal craft for family fun on rivers and lakes, offers a thrilling experience when used on the ocean's surf. The cushioned craft is very safe in all types of water, and offers an easy way to teach children their first lessons in water enjoyment.

In fishing, surfing, camping, or shooting whitewater, the canoe reaches places otherwise inaccessible. It can be backpacked or motorbiked upstream and floated down, and should the paddling technique go awry, it doesn't matter whether you go sideways or backwards, the craft doesn't tip, but rides like a cork, right side up.

When small rafts are used, 2 or 3 are often tied together to increase security.

## THE RAFTING BREED

Beyond the rivers, and the craft to negotiate them, what about the people who float their courses? One main reason people run rivers is to learn the meaning of real wilderness. The wild rivers provide a natural access to unspoiled regions of rare beauty and scenic grandeur. They offer a unique blend of excitement and relaxation as you dash down a rapid or drift with calm current. You discover a freedom in wilderness that relieves the stresses of modern living. Floating with the timeless rhythm of a river develops an appreciation of the natural order of things, new attitudes toward the environment, and a rewarding learning experience. Thus, the wild river, whose origin is lost in antiquity, brings deep concepts (akin to religion) to a man—especially the concept of his littleness in the "Grand Plan."

## TOUR ORGANIZATION AND LEADERSHIP

Rafting expeditions are sponsored by several organizations and many commercial operators. All are forever vigilant for the rafters' safety, which includes advance scouting of rivers for hazards, precise scheduling, and instruction. The Western Rivers Guides Associations set safety standards for their memberships. Cooperation, rather than competition, among river guides includes sharing knowledge about equipment and seasonal characteristics of currents.

*The American River Touring Association* (1016 Jackson St, Oakland, California, 94607), called ARTA, is a non-profit educational association, whose purposes include:

1. Teaching the basic skills necessary to safely enjoy our wilderness waterways, rivers, lakes, and seacoasts.

2. Teaching people to protect adjacent shores.

3. Publishing information, describing routes, access areas, campsites, points of interest, and facilities along the way.

4. Conducting trips which demonstrate the pleasures of river touring and shore camping.

In addition to sponsoring stateside trips, ARTA has embarked on a global program of bringing to people experiences on far-flung waterways. Typical are the two trips scheduled for January, 1972. One is for 8½ days down the Rio Patuca River in Honduras, traveling over 500 miles through lush, green, and scenic primitive jungle. The other is scheduled for Australia's Great Barrier Reef, Queensland and Fiji in a 29-day expedition, organized as follows: 1 day air travel each way; 10 days of cruising the ocean through Whitsunday Passage, island hopping from Hayman to Lindeman, the Molle Group, and many other romantic islands; 11 days for a land expedition to Mount Cootha, overlooking the scenic city of Brisbane, Lamington National Park for leisurely hikes through cool bushlands by mountain streams and waterfalls; and 6 days for a visit to Fiji for a land and Nasekaw River expedition on bamboo rafts, camping in an isolated Figian village, then continuing to the sea.

For experienced young men and women, ARTA offers a Paddle Option on stateside floats, in which participants engage in a more active involvement with the river, paddling much of the determined course.

*The Sierra Club* (1050 Mills Tower, San Francisco, California, 94104), a pioneer organization for users of the wilderness, was founded by John Muir in 1892 "to help people explore, enjoy, and protect parks, wilderness, waters, forests, and wildlife," conducts a variety of raft trips.

*The Wilderness Society* (2144 P Street, N. W., Washington, D.C.), specifically devoted to increasing knowledge and appreciation of the wilderness and establishing policies for its protection and use, also offers rafting experiences.

Tour operators, with competent guides knowledgeable in the ways of wild rivers and in the techniques of handling people, include:

*River Trips*, 802 University Ave., Laramie, Wyoming, 82070.

*Canyonlands Expeditions, Inc.*, P. O. Box 21021, Salt Lake City, Utah, 84121.

*Hatch River Expeditions*, 411 E. 200 N., Vernal, Utah, 84078.

*Holiday River Expeditions, Inc.*, 519 Malibu Drive, Salt Lake City, Utah, 84121.

*Moki Mac River Expeditions*, 6829 Bella Vista Drive, Salt Lake City, Utah, 84121.

*North American River Runners, Inc.*, 570 North Main Street, Moab, Utah, 84532.

*Tex's Tour Center*, P. O. Box 67, Moab, Utah, 84532.

*Western River Expeditions, Inc.*, P. O. Box 6339, Salt Lake City, Utah, 84106.

*Wonderland Expeditions*, 3863 South 825 West, Bountiful, Utah, 84010.

*Frontier Airline* (Stapleton Airport, Denver, Colorado, 80207) and the *Hub Air Flying Service* (Canyonlands Airport, Moab, Utah, 84532) are other sources for river tours and combination raft-jeep tours.

*Trip Information* On most river trips, members camp along the shore, the only exception being the Rogue River trip in Oregon, where lodging is available. Shedding the veneer of civilization with kindred folk, rafting trip rosters include politicians, school teachers, judges, bank presidents, lawyers, executives, professors, mothers, and children. Trips range from 1 to 8 days, and 4 to 5 hours are spent on the river each day. You can choose a trip that's suitable for a 10-year old child, or a 70-year-old grandparent, and participate in complete confidence that all will return unscathed. Your tour host will designate all gear, and schedule information. As a general yardstick of cost, various trips range from $10 to $50 per day.

## ECOLOGY

Humans attempting to relate to their environment through outdoor activities can sometimes encounter tragic results. In pursuit of credibility, it must be reported that tragedies have occurred in rafting wild rivers.

During the third week of June, 1970, 4 groups, totaling 45 people, in 7 rafts and 2 wooden McKenzie River boats, floated the middle fork of Idaho's Salmon River, which, because of flood-caused high water, produced waves that stood, in some stretches, 30' in the air. The popular route of 113 miles to the main stream of the Salmon is usually run in a 5-day float, and during that span of time in June, 1970, 4 persons (3 adults and 1 teen-ager) lost their lives. It is no consolation to know that old-time rivermen claim these drownings were the first ever to result from rafting accidents on the middle fork.

Lou Slagowski, administrative assistant of the Salmon National Forest, acted promptly to issue warnings, through newspapers, radio and TV stations, that the water conditions were extremely dangerous, and urged rafting parties to wait until the high water dropped. He believes strongly that permits should be required, for the sake of better control, and to enable the Forest Service to prohibit river floats completely in times of high risk.

A year later, in June, 1971, a Boy Scout drowned in the Green River (southern Utah) when rubber rafts collided with floating logs, dislodging the passengers. Leaders and 22 Scouts made it safely to shore and were rescued by heliocopters.

Steve Strong, of the Utah Travel Council, commenting on the tragedy, said, ". . . this section of the Green . . . is wilderness . . . . It's a rough river, wild, and during high water, occasionally dangerous. The Utah Travel Council always recommends that the people sign on with a reputable river running company, and never try to tackle the Green (or any Utah river) alone."

Shooting any rapid, in any boat, where the fast-moving, high-velocity craft can meet a stationary object—cliff, jagged rock, or fallen tree—is dangerous. The boat may be unable to swing completely around, or away and free, or could be ripped and/or completely engulfed, sweeping off passengers and gear. The power of surging water is titanic, and experienced outdoorsmen are ever vigilant and highly respectful of this force in nature.

## BUYER'S GUIDE

**Canoe/Kayak Sources**
Seylor (see Kayak Corporation, page 131) inflated canoes have remarkable stability, and can be used on the ocean as well as on rivers and lakes. They are constructed of Neopryl, a new material of PVC and synthetic rubber, electronically welded under high frequency. Neither sun, saltwater, or chlorine affects the material. All boats except the K-26 are delivered with carrying bag and repair kit.

The K-26 is probably the smallest canoe available with its 4'4" x 23" size and weight of 4 pounds.
Price: $20.00.
The K-37 measures 5'7" x 28" and weighs 7 pounds.
Price: $35.00.
The K-56 measures 7' x 30" and weighs 9 pounds.
Price: $50.00.
The above 3 models are for adults as well as for children. All have built-in removable air mattresses, 5 independent air chambers, and bow and stern spray covers.

The K-50 Banana Boat measures 8'6" x 36" and weighs 15 pounds. It is a 2-man canoe with 2 air chambers, lifelines attached to the bow and stern, and built-in drain plug. The raised ends assure dry riding in high waves.
Price: $70.00.

*An ARTA sponsored wild white-water trip in one of the numerous wilderness rivers in the West*

The K-67 Tahiti measures 9'6" x 3' and weighs 18 pounds. This 2-man canoe has an inflatable backrest, built-in inflatable floor, bow and stern spray covers, and 8 independent air chambers.

Price: $75.00.

The K-77 Tahiti measures 11' x 34", weighs 20 pounds, and has the same equipment as the K-67, except for the number of air chambers (11 instead of 8).

Price: $100.00.

Accessories for Sevylor canoes: foot pump, $2.25; 7' double-bladed, 3 sectional paddle, $7.50; 4'4" double-bladed baby paddle for model K-26, $4.00.

**Aigle Hutchinson** (see Kayak Corporation, page 131) offers a versatile canoe in Surf-Rider, which measures 10'6" x 2'11", weighs 30 pounds; and can be paddled or sailed. Built-in, permanently anchored inflatable floor provides maximum stability and is capable of holding 2 adults plus gear up to 500 pounds.

Price: $175.00; with 26 square foot sail, mast, and rudder, $235.00.

Accessories: double-bladed sectional paddle, $16; drift sail, 16 square feet, $18.

**Leisure Imports** (see page 127) offers various inflated canoes.

All craft in the Leisure line are orange in color. Carrying bag and repair kit are included in the prices. All items are guaranteed for one year against defective material and/or workmanship.

The N-1 model measures 6'3" x 2'4", weighs 7 pounds, and has a 200-pound capacity. The 6 separate air compartments are capable of supporting 1 teen-ager or 2 children.

Price: $39.95.

The N-2 model measures 7'6" x 2'5", weighs 12 pounds, and has a 250-pound capacity. The 6 separate air compartments are capable of supporting 1 adult or 2 children.

Price: $54.95.

The N-4 model measures 9'6" x 2'9", weighs 17 pounds, has a 450-pound capacity, and is capable of seating 2 adults. It has 9 separate air compartments, and a removable inflated seat.

Price: $79.95.

The N-5 model measures 10'8" x 3'1", weighs 20 pounds, has a 550-pound capacity, and is capable of accommodating 2 adults. This craft has 11 separate air compartments and two removable seats.

Price: $99.95.

Accessories: 6 foot double-bladed paddle, $5.99; 8 foot double-bladed paddle, $9.99; rubber pump, $1.99; extra seat, $9.99.

**Recreonics** (see page 130) offers the Tahiti K37 and the Tahiti K57.

Tahiti K37, 6'3" x 2'4", the smallest model in the line, includes features similar to K57.

Price: $30.00.

Tahiti K57, 7'6" x 2'6", includes 5 air chambers, backrest, inflatable floor, spray covers, repair kit and carrying bag, for the solo rider.

Price: $48.00.

**River Rafts**

**Inflatable Boats Unlimited** (P. O. Box 21021, Salt Lake City, Utah, 84121), which offers eight models of river-running rafts, is probably the only source other than the rapidly diminishing surplus army sale.

All inflatables in the line are constructed of 3 fabrics, made to military specifications: 24 oz. neoprene-impregnated ripstop nylon, and 48 oz., and 64 oz. neoprene-impregnated nylon.

D-rings are included with all rafts, and many options and accessories are available.

Sportyak is a 7-foot, 1-man, river model.
Price: $275.00.

Selway is a 12-foot model. It is built like a 7-man military assault raft and modified for whitewater use.
Price: $495.00.

Rio Grande is a 12-foot model for 6 passengers.
Price: $445.60.

Yampa is a 15'7" model that is designed and built to military specifications and similar to 10-man assault raft.
Price: $655.43.

Zeebird, a 16' model, has a V-bottom for motorized cruising.
Price: $1,330.00.

Snake, an 18' model, is used by most commercial operators on the Snake River.
Price: $1,475.00.

Salmon, a 20' model, is new to the company's line.
Price: $1,132.00.

Colorado is designed specifically for the Grand Canyon. It is available in 22', 27', 33', and 37' lengths.
Price: $2,345.60.

# 15. THE AIRBOAT

The airboat, it seems, is to the South what the snowmobile is to the North—an excellent example of man using a specialized vehicle on unique local terrain for recreation and service. The airboat enables the adventuring man to reach once inaccessible places—saw grass prairies, saltwater marshes, and swamps—where the merger of water, vegetation, and wetland formerly prevented him from using the conventional boat, swamp buggy, or wading boots.

The creation of the airboat came in the late 1930s and since then it has spread to all parts of the world. The popularity of the craft is steadily rising, especially among all types of outdoorsmen, government agencies, corporations, and foreign governments.

The use of an airboat opens up prolific hunting grounds by transporting big game hunters into the backswamps of the South and the muskeg country in Alaska. Fishermen everywhere can be transported to isolated water that cannot be reached in any other way. Many of the frog legs appearing on restaurant menus come from that segment of southern hunters who use the airboat for nocturnal hunts to spear the frogs.

Airboat racing, as an organized activity, has little popularity, but Earl Dixon of Miami claims that the first airboat race was held in 1952 in Cooperstown, Florida. The hardy contestants risked the loss of an arm, for the early boats had no prop guards and had to be cranked by hand.

## DESCRIPTION OF THE AIRBOAT

The airboat is essentially little more than a rectangular-shaped, scow-type boat, but the airplane motor and propeller placed above the rearward make it a fast and efficient craft for its purpose, skimming over the varied conditions of semi-solid terrain. Until a few years ago, the airboat was a do-it-yourself project but now, a few companies offer factory-made jobs that sport a streamline design, sophisticated engineering, and extended use, as over snow and ice.

The standard size hull is 6' x 12', made of .001 sheet aluminum (approximately ⅛ of an inch). Some airboat hulls are made of fiberglass or a combination of varied materials such as wooden sides and aluminum bottom. The power unit is an airplane motor ranging on the average from 100 to 125 hp and capable of propelling the craft from 35 to 40 mph. The airplane motors most favored by airboat makers include the Lycoming, Continental, and Franklin. Up to the late 1960s, all airboats were handcrafted by individuals, and a custom-built boat with the above specifications cost from $1,800 to $2,400. An airboat with a 7' x 16' hull and 345 hp engine that is able to clock 72 mph (without load) can cost as much as $5,000.

Many owners, veterans who know the back trails, discover that airboats are intriguing to tourists, and commercial sightseeing rides are a spinoff from purely personal use.

The airboat's creation, much like the dune buggy's, is mostly relegated to the garage mechanic, who constructs it to individual specifications, shape, and overall design. However, certain standards seem to be universal: a strong broad hull, metal superstructure for mounting the engine which is disposed rearward, a single or double rudder, and controls.

**Hull**   Airboat do-it-yourselfers have built hulls from tin, aluminum, stainless steel, fiberglass, plywood, cypress, mahogany, and teakwood. Rigid

metal makes the fabrication of suitable chine (contoured bottom to enhance stability) difficult, and after rough use, the welds in metal or rivets in aluminum may jar loose. Flexible hull (fiberglass) adherents frown upon the rigid metal hull. The rectangular boxy hull, with dimensions, over and under, of 6' x 12' x 12", has an upswept bow to enable the craft to ride over dense vegetation. Sometimes a saw grass rake is added. This is a superstructure of metal piping or strips that are attached as an extension of the upward sweep of the bow, to ride better over tall weeds. Some builders cover the bow portion with a deck to prevent wind drag and stop plant debris from falling into the boat.

**Engine**   Popular airplane engines include the Continental and Franklin, which cost approxi-

*A typical airboat with standard size hull and fiberglass construction*

mately $400 used and $1,900 to $2,500 new. Lycoming engines are more expensive; the 125 hp engine costs $1,475 used and $3,060 new. In order to economize, some people use a snowmobile-type engine: a JLO LR-440/2, 36 hp power plant costs $345 and the 50 hp model costs $695.

The propeller is a pusher type that directs the air past the rudder surfaces for more sensitive control. Its position above the transom gives more room in the boat's hull. Propeller guards are constructed of ½" and ¾" steel tubing and are covered with a 2" or 4" wire mesh.

The engines are supported on stands fabricated from 1" and 1¼" square tubing, the size depending on the weight of the engine, which must be set dead center in perfect alignment. Balance and stability in airboats are involved with a different principle from that of conventional boats. The thrust line of an airboat is above the center of gravity, a line through the center of the propeller, and it tends to force the bow down. The conventional boat's thrust line through the underwater prop is below the center of gravity which forces the bow upward. This simply means that to start the airboat from a standing position, a full throttle to send the prop at 2,700 rpm is necessary.

**Rudders** As there is no keel to the airboat, the 1 or 2 rudders, placed immediately aft of the spinning prop, determine control in steering. There is some skidding on sharp turns. The rudders generally carry the identifying registration numbers, painted 10 inches high on their sides. If the airboat is to be used in open waters (lakes or channels), regular marine equipment laws for small boats are followed: fire extinguisher, life preservers, running lights (top white at night), and a flag on a pole 10 feet high (so that its presence can be spotted in high grass).

The steering system is activated by a flexible push-pull cable leading to the rudder assembly from the steering wheel. The greater the speed, the more sensitive is the airboat to change of direction.

**Controls** The simple, overall characteristics of the airboat do not require complicated wiring or instrumentation. Controls consist of a starting (key) switch, throttle control of engine and propeller speed, and rudder controls.

**General** Some airboats have windshields, most do not. The pilot sits solo in most boats, though some have a 2 and 3 seat capacity affording the long view for passengers. Airboat fuel is aviation gasoline, which is available at boat marinas. Depending on the horsepower of the engine and cruising conditions, 3 to 5 gallons of gas are used per hour. Airboats with a tuned muffler make no more noise than a 2-cycle motorcycle or ATV.

The airboat qualifies as an all-season boat; there's no underwater propeller, rudder, or keel to snag on rocks or weeds, and it skims over wet grass, sandbars, mud, marsh, snow, ice, and tundra.

THE DRIVING AND RIDING EXPERIENCE

Before starting the engine, the pilot always looks back to see that all is clear around the propeller and behind the craft. During the warmup, the engine must be gunned. This offsets the resistance of the hull in water and grass by giving a surge of power which gets the hull planing upward and over the restraining forces. A bow that rides deep plows into the water and places extreme strain on the engine. Once underway, the roar from the gunned engine is deafening, and conversation is nonexistent. Some passengers use ear plugs to deaden the sound of the engine.

As in most vehicles where the passengers sit low to the ground, the airboat seems to be going faster than it really is. In the low seat position, the wind only inches above the hull's bottom, whistles past your ears and your stomach flutters as you are transported to new adventures.

Skimming along, driver and passengers must be careful with loose materials that may be sucked into the propeller, in many cases, shattering it. Hats, rain gear, plastic bags, lunch boxes, sunglasses, paddles, loose tackle, and tools must be secured when the engine is running.

In airboat country, you'll be involved most with the tall grass that is pushed down by the craft and the boat's vibration when dry, uneven terrain is encountered. The vast marshland with its profuse growth and the spooked, squeaking birds will offer ever-changing visual and auditory stimuli. The shimmering saw grass, wood ibis, cormorants, eagles, ospreys, coots, great white and blue herons, and varied ducks create an animate and wild landscape—the type hard to come by in this age of the bulldozer and cement mixer.

First-time pilots should remember that the airboat will not turn as rapidly in mud as it will in more resistant grass and soil conditions. The fact that the bottom of an airboat is usually flat causes it to go into a skid on turns, sometimes flipping the pilot and running wild. Many veterans, sometimes injured, have spent the night in a swamp until they were rescued the next day. Skidding and loss of control, in most instances, is prevented by backing off the throttle and easing up on turns.

As a beginning airboater, be careful when traveling over mud flats since they can bog you down. Once you stop, the mud flats are very much like quicksand. Try to keep moving so that the hull has no time to settle in the suction pad type of terrain. However, in practically every other compatible terrain condition, the airboat (being air propelled and without protrusions under the hull) need not depend on conventional traction for progress.

After operating the airboat in salt marshes or seawater, always hose it down inside and out before storing it away. The entire hull should also be checked for scratches, deep gouges, loose seams, or rivets.

## AREAS OF USE

For some outdoorsmen, the airboat has replaced the pole boat in east Texas, Mississippi, and the Gulf Coast, and also the pirogue in the bayou country of Louisiana. In North and South Carolina and Virginia, the airboat is used inland and on coastal wetlands. Men have brought their airboats to Wyoming, Wisconsin, Michigan, and stretches of the Mississippi River for outdoor recreation—mostly fishing.

**Georgia** The Okefenokee Swamp (sometimes called the "Dismal Swamp") in southeast Georgia, offers many thousands of acres of wet prairies and exotic scenery. First-time visitors are surprised to discover that the swamp is not all dismal. Actually, a large part of the land is composed of expansive savannahs which offer a unique type of scenery, indescribably different and beautiful. The untouched, primitive portions of the swamp are available to the airboat operator, who can drive over an interesting blend of grass and water.

**Florida** The sport of airboating is probably most popular in Florida. Its fabled "River of Grass" is an extensive 5,000 square mile wilderness, the only subtropical area in the nation. It extends in a wide dimension from Lake Okeechobee to the Gulf of Mexico. The southern portion is set aside as Everglades National Park. The wild land is covered with water to a depth of 18" in some places, always moving and fluctuating with the weather cycles; high during the subtropical heavy downpours of summer, low during the dry season. The long views are broken up by hummocks where the land is built up like giant flower pots to heights of 3 to 4 feet and supports trees up to 30 feet tall. The true value of experiencing the Everglades comes when the airboater and his party stop, shut off the engine, allow the disrupted area to return to silence, and with their eyes explore the sky, land, and water, then celebrate with a picnic lunch.

For further information contact:
*Florida Airboat Association*, Fran Taylor, 1624 W. 33rd Place, Hialeah, Florida, 33000.

## RECREATION USES

The broad recreational use of the airboat reaches all ages for opportunities to view the rare sights of the Everglades in Florida, salt marshes in coastal states, and bayou county in the deep South. Hunting, fishing, frogging, bird and animal watching, and photography reach new dimensions with the airboat, and the participant is rewarded with sights, feelings, and activities seldom experienced by the sidewalk man.

**Hunting and Fishing Camps** An airboat guide, Curtis Head, of Homossasa Springs, Florida, estimates that the airboat, in his area, is used 75 percent for hunting, 10 percent for fishing, 10 percent for frogging, and 5 percent for orchid collecting and bird watching. Airboat owners combine into groups or clubs to construct a permanent camp-shack, bunks, and kitchen which are used as a base of operations for fishing the isolated potholes, ponds, canals, and streams for bass, snook, tarpon and bream and speckled bass.

In the hunting season, the quarry can include: deer, bear, raccoon, wild boar, and other regional animals. The camps offer facilities for dressing out the game, and even freezing it in some well-furnished camps.

Between seasons, besides repairing or enlarging the camp, some sportsmen plant gardens

*The airboat qualifies as an all-season boat; it skims over wet grass, sandbars, mud, marsh, snow, ice, and tundra.*

which grow turnips, tomatoes, potatoes, and collards up to 23″ across!

Evenings are made tolerable with the use of a compressor and fogging gun to spray malathion vapor; an effective measure to dispatch all flying and creeping pests.

(Note: In Florida the airboat license costs $6.00 for which the state Game Department grants an operator's permit. The airboat users, with other proper licenses, are allowed to gig frogs, shoot game, and catch fish.)

**Frogging** "Frog legs" on a restaurant menu represent, for many, a gourmet favorite—cold frog legs with lemon mayonnaise, breaded with light cracker crumbs, sauteed in butter, etc. One method of capturing frogs is wading with high top tennis shoes, hip boots, or waders. The canoe

and johnboat are also used, but the most rewarding way is by use of the airboat.

The 2 sizeable frogs of the southland are speared by the hunter, while going approximately 20 mph, steering the boat, reaching out with the long pole and gigging the frog without stopping the airboat. The frogs are impaled on the barbed tip, lifted up, pulled off the gig, and dropped into a chute at the side of the driver's seat. A wetted gunny sack, attached to the bottom of the chute, serves as a storage bag.

Frogging is done mostly at night. The equipment consists of a battery-operated head lamp (to keep both hands free) with a strong concentrated beam that dimly reflects the eyes of the frog and an 8′ to 10′ pole with a barbed gig at the end. There are 2 popular types of gig on the market; one with prongs arranged in a circular pattern, the other with 3 prongs in a straight line (a miniature version of the fish spear).

The frogging trip often keeps the hunter out all night, and in the past, commercial froggers have bagged as many as 600 frogs in one night. Frogs generally weigh less than 8 ounces, and cleaned, packed in a plastic bag and frozen, they command $2 per pound in the gourmet marketplace.

**Photography** A camera can add another dimension to airboating satisfaction. Photography is an activity many hunters have embraced—camera shooting instead of gun shooting safaris or outings. The airboat takes the photographer to remote and uninhabited areas that offer a shooter's dream in the variety of flora, bird, and wildlife: palm trees, isolated pine and cypress trees, and the myriad of bright flowers; birds flying solo or in flocks, skimmers sailing low in search of unwary minnows, swallowtail kites in graceful flight, the awkward-looking anhinga preening his feathers, the stately heron, and the regal eagle, our endangered national bird; otters playing on mud banks, the raccoon capturing cray fish or collecting oysters that cling to the mangrove roots, alligators, fox, deer, and even the panther that prowls deep in wooded areas.

When hunting with a camera, there are no licenses required, no seasons, no bag limits, or any type of limitation on the game you shoot.

**Nature Observation** Once deep in a Florida

*Airboat marina in Florida, where airboating is probably the most popular*

saw-grass prairie, you shut off your airboat motor and man-made noise is replaced with silence— broken only by the haunting cries of marsh birds and the frogs, deep and resonate piglike grunts. You are only a temporary intruder in a mysterious world known only to the Seminole Indians, National Park rangers, and an occasional naturalist or scientist.

You take in the panorama of grass savannahs, which unroll from horizon to horizon and change in mood with each hour, each season, and each year, and you soon realize that you are witnessing a rich ecosystem. No matter how many times you visit, there are always different experiences to make a nature lover out of the most blah city resident.

## SERVICE USES

Airboats are not limited to recreation. They serve man in many climes from the Amazon to the Arctic in diverse services: for rescue missions in floods; for rescue of lost persons or downed planes; for removing deer from flooded areas; and for transporting surveyors, oil explorers, missionaries, rangers, and government personnel (such as the Corps of Engineers, Department of Agriculture, and the Bureau of Sport Fisheries) to remote places.

Airboats permit large cargoes and shorten the time of travel to remote and difficult land and water areas. They transport exploring equipment and instruments, food and medicine, and firefighting and mosquito-abatement apparatus. They take the sick to hospitals, and carry soldiers in Vietnam. The airboat is known to all geographical areas of the world: Alaska, Canada, South America, Africa, the Philippine Islands, and Vietnam.

## IMPACT ON ECOLOGY

Man, with his airboat, receives a fair report card. As with other vehicle owners, the "bad apples" get the publicity and hurt the majority. Users of airboats that ply the prolific marshlands have been accused of destroying the habitats of wildlife and of poaching alligators and other animals. The taking of alligators, which is illegal at all times, represents a lucrative project to the poacher. That they are poached is attested to by commercial frog hunters, sensitive to the conditions of their hunting grounds, who inform that

years ago they would observe 40 to 50 alligators in a night's hunt; today, they rarely see more than 3 or 4. The poachers, along with other forces, have greatly diminished the alligator population—to the brink of extinction.

In the drought that parched the Everglades during the first 4 months of 1971, many wildfires burned for weeks, the smoke and ashes reaching Miami, disrupting traffic, and delaying a national golf tournament. The fires were attributed to persons traversing the dry land in airboats, swamp buggies, and half-tracks, and led to an order by the Florida Game and Fresh Water Fish Commission that banned the vehicles from the area. Permanent destruction to marshland occurs when a fire burns like charcoal or peat, drying out the moisture and burning on, tunneling down and laterally along the bedrock. This condition completely sterilizes the land and makes it worthless. As with humus in a forest, the rich Everglade muckland (up to 5 feet deep) took centuries to accumulate. All in all, the conditions that wrought destruction to the Everglades serve as a warning to the recreationist to be forever vigilant in safeguarding the land and its creatures.

In the conservationist's concern about airboats riding over the nurseries of birds and animals, mashing down their delicate havens, it is to be noted that many airboats traversing a given area do less damage than claimed. Most use marked trails, as it would be foolhardy to set out blindly into unmarked wilderness areas where breakdowns and accidents may occur.

Robert Ritsch of the Bureau of Outdoor Recreation, Washington, D.C. engaged in a study to ascertain the extent of destruction caused by airboats in the Everglades. Sections of heavy use, showing many tracks, were fenced off, prohibiting all use for 4 months. After that period, an inspection of the controlled area with Major Louis Gainey indicated little or no damage. Ritsch reported, "Wildlife, water birds, deer, raccoons, snakes, and alligators were abundant, even though people have been hunting the area for the last 35 to 40 years."

John C. Jones, president of the Florida Wildlife Federation, indicates that his Federation ". . . is attempting to organize all the sportsmen in south Florida (the Everglades) to make better sportsmen and conservationists. There are very few of these sportsmen who are guilty of irresponsible acts, but of course the innocent must suffer because of the actions of a few."

Observations indicate that the majority of airboat owners are seasoned outdoorsmen. They have a deep respect for the delicate land they use and a conservation consciousness that they strive to inculcate on others.

True, man comes first, but not to the extent of destroying and eliminating his natural inheritance. The marshlands, as many other areas with unique ecosystems, are so rare that they demand special treatment, for once despoiled, they are irreplaceable. We inherited them all—to use, enjoy, explore, study, and pass on to our children's children.

## BUYER'S GUIDE

Few companies manufacture complete, ready-to-use airboats. Two firms in Florida sell their products in all parts of the world, where they are used by the military, oil and construction companies, and various government agencies.

**Hurricane Fiberglass Products Corp.** (Box 8, Lake Hamilton, Florida, 33851) offers 3 Tomcats and 4 Aircats.

The Tomcat models are similar in length of hull, 10'; beam, 5'; depth amidship, 16''; and in details of engine stand, rudder, gas tank, propeller, and guard. The engines range from 36 hp to 50 hp. The total weight ranges from 285 to 350 pounds.

JLO Rockwell, 2-cycle engines are used in Tomcats and Tomcats are claimed to be the easiest vehicle to operate because of the single joystick and simple movements: a twist on the top of the handle to accelerate or slow down; move the handle left to go left; and move the handle right to go right.

Price: model 1/36, $995; model 11/50, $1,495; model 11, $1,620.

The Aircat models range in length from 14' to 17'; beam, 6'4'' to 7'2''; depth amidship, 22'' to 24''; hp, 125 to 180; cruise speed, 45 to 55 mph; and carrying capacity, 700 to 1,100 pounds.

All Aircats have the following features: all fiberglass construction, catamaran design, push-button start, generator or alternator, running lights, electric gauges, and a recording tachometer. The high forward operator's seat is included for added visibility

and protection when running through dense vegetation. Special camouflaging colors are available without extra cost.

Prices: model 14/125, $3,480; model 14/150, $3,850; model 14/180, $4,250; and model 17/180, $5,550.

Since 1947, Tomcats and Aircats have been used throughout the world by Alaskan and Mexican hunters, Canadian wildlife conservationists, Colombian fish biologists, East Pakistanian missionaries, and Venezuelan farmers, among others.

**Mid Florida Aluminum Corp.** (1339 W. Washington St., Orlando, Florida, 32800) offers a line of AirGator airboats including the Pathfinder, 13'; Trailblazer, 13'; Explorer, 15'; and Ranger, 18'. All have a beam of 84''. The power comes from 4-cylinder and 6-cylinder Franklin aircraft engines, capable of putting out 130 hp and 220 hp respectively. The top of the line, the Ranger is a commercial model with the 220 hp engine and is capable of carrying 3,000 pounds of cargo.

All models are factory made from aluminum alloy in all-weld, no-rivet construction. Flotation is built-in, and all models are built like a sports car. There is a minimum of cornering slide, and a soft safe ride is claimed. The company set their own high standards for smoothness and quietness, with the flexibility of high-torque, low-end acceleration, and effortless high rpm speeds.

AirGator's proving grounds are Florida's endless miles of swamps, lakes, rivers, and canals, and all models proved to be equally at home "on a heavy dew" as in deep water.

**Susquehanna Air Motors** (5217 Terrace Road, Mechanicsburg, Pennsylvania, 17055) offers a portable air motor that can be applied to any suitable small boat (10' to 16') and can be driven at a 10 mph clip.

Price: $249.95.

**Banks-Maxwell** (Box 3301, Ft. Worth, Texas, 76105) offers kits, plans, propellers, supplies, and converted engines (Corvair and VW) in 90, 125, 150, and 220 hp.

**Fran Taylor** (1624 W. 33rd Place, Hialeah, Florida, 33000) offers complete facilities to fabricate any type of airboat the customer chooses. He has built more airboats probably than any other individual in the United States.

# 16. THE CANOE

An Indian creation, par excellence, the canoe is a picturesque and functional craft, steeped in American exploration history and romanticized in the literature of our continent. Somewhere in time—thousands of years ago—in the dim pine and hemlock forests of the continent, aborigine craftsmen fashioned the frame of the bark-covered canoe.

Through the centuries, various Indian artisans, independently and cooperatively, made contributions to the rib bending and forming, keel setting, rocker shaping, bark covering, stitching, and gumming of the ever-evolving, ever-improving, bark canoe.

When the white man came upon the North American scene, the bark canoes had developed to such perfection in design, construction, and function, that he embraced the craft without alteration and used it extensively to explore, to engage in fur trading, and to discover and eventually settle approximately a quarter of the New World.

Today, even in the Space Age, the basic design of a canoe still stands and is still used—a gift from those craftsmen in the dim forests.

## MODERN CANOES

The functional values and safety features of the modern canoe embody the original features: pointed at both ends, broad beam, upward sweep of bow and stern, etc. The modern craft, as did its Indian counterpart, efficiently and silently parts the water, pushing it aside and permitting it to return to the stern without wake or disturbance. The low draft enables it to skim on the top of the water without plowing, and a single paddle stroke sends it effectively along.

The fabric skin of the modern canoe has included such coverings as papier-mâché, molded rubber, and cedar planking; however, 3 basic types are most used: fabric (canvas, Dacron, etc.) over wood, aluminum, and fiberglass.

The square stern for attachment of motor is offered, though not popular since most canoeists prefer to maintain the original shape. Should power be needed, a side-mounted bracket is attached.

**Sizes** Canoes under 16' are mainly used solo, serving well for youngsters on small bodies of calm water and for adults involved in hunting and fishing projects. These craft can be carried to remote potholes and other inaccessible places. Recently released, the smallest model commercially available is the Rushton Pack Canoe, slightly over 10' long and weighing only 18.5 pounds.

Canoes in the 16', 17', and 18' class immediately add greater advantages of stability, strength, and greater passenger and cargo

*Bow River, which flows through the mountains of Banff National Park, offers ideal canoeing waters.*

capacity. The 16-footer seats 2 comfortably, usually weighs less than 65 pounds, and has a carrying capacity of 1,000 pounds. The 17-footer, weighing approximately 75 pounds, supports 2 paddlers and 1 passenger, and is considered the best all-round size for leisurely cruising and extended tripping. The 18-footer is ideal for wilderness camping and service uses where heavy loads and passengers (up to 5) must be carried.

**Keel** Most canoes have a keel, which gives them a stiff spine and helps to protect their bottoms. On flat water, the keel abets paddling on a straight course. The canoe without keel is used in fast-moving water for better maneuverability, quicker response, and sidewise movement and to avoid or slide over rock and log obstructions.

**Paddles** Factory-made, mass-produced paddles, fashioned from one piece of hardwood, as maple or ash, are satisfactory for the beginner. In selection, the stern paddle should measure up to the user's eyes; the bow paddle, to the user's chin. However, arm span varies among individuals of the same height, so paddle length can vary. Select one long enough to allow the submerging of the entire blade while stroking without awkward leaning or reaching. The canoeist, with increasing experience, will probably consider the laminated paddle, which is hand-crafted by gluing a blade of several pieces of spruce, fir, cedar, or basswood to a stout shaft. The laminates are light and whippy, ideal for open water paddling.

**Accessories** Although there is versatility in the canoe, per se, many accessories are available for specialized use, comfort, safety, and decor. They include pontoons to enhance stability in rough water, outboard motor bracket, motors (3 hp or less), rowing attachment, yokes for carrying, specialized paddles, bang strips (to protect the bow), cushions, backrest, dunnage bags, folding crew seat, floorboards, gunwale covers, sailing rigs, anchor, cartop carrier, tie-downs, whitewater helmet, decals, decorative strips, and repair kit.

## ACQUIRING CANOE SKILLS

Consider the learn-to-swim process of very young children. He or she first runs on the beach, splashing the ankle-deep water, amid shouts and screams; then they wade into deeper water, splash themselves and their companions. This is usually followed by ducking the face under water, then submerging completely, holding the nose during the new experience. Next, is laying out on the water and dog paddling. Later, the kick comes into play. Thus, youngsters, in varying degree of progress, become oriented to the new-found element, gain confidence, and are on their way to becoming adequate swimmers.

Similarly, techniques in canoeing can evolve quite naturally. As a rank amateur (of any age), take a companion with swim suits and life preservers to a shallow and placid river or lake, board, and begin paddling. Both paddlers stroke rhythmically together on opposite sides of the canoe. Note the quick response of the craft to the newcomer's movements of the paddle. Then both paddlers leave their seats, kneel on the floor of the canoe, and paddle from that position.

Change positions and you will note that the confined quarters of the bow position (where the craft tapers to a point) do not allow much confidence at first, while the stern position gives a spacious and stable-appearing view of the entire canoe. You will soon discover that unlike vehicles which steer from the front, it is the stern paddler, to a large degree, who determines steering and control in a canoe.

Gliding along with straight pull strokes, you soon become aware of a slight deviation to the left (for right-handed stern paddlers), which comes from the stern paddler's advantage of longer stroke and canoe design (tapering to the rear). A compensating J movement flip with the paddle blade at the end of the stroke keeps the craft on a straight course.

Stopping the forward progress (jam stroke) is a matter of slicing the paddle blade (perpendicular to the keel) downward into the water alongside the gunwale. The canoe's forward progress stopped, try a few back strokes, then draw strokes (pullover and pushover) to move the canoe sideways. Practice forward and reverse sweeps to turn or pivot the canoe.

Continue to experiment. Slice the paddle blade diagonally away from the canoe, turn it and pull the flat side of the blade toward you. Next, push the flat side of the blade outward, turn, and slice it back. Try moving the blade back and forth in a path parallel to the canoe side at an angle that will give a propeller effect and move the canoe sideways.

These get-acquainted paddle movements have the basic elements of all strokes—even if you don't know the names of each. For complete information on basic cruising and advanced stroking skills, see Chapters 7 and 8 of Malo's *Complete Guide to Canoeing and Canoe-Camping* (New York: Collier Books, 1970).

Practice changing seat positions, first by the improper method of standing upright and walking along: you'll notice an instability. But, in the proper, bent-over position, with the hands sliding along the gunwales, there is no unsteadiness and little danger of falling out.

Next, one participant should leave the canoe, grasp it at the stern end and push it along, using a frog or flutter kick. Then, from the amidships position, he should grasp the gunwale and rock the canoe gently at first, then violently, so that the passenger remaining aboard experiences stability features from various positions: sitting on the seat, sitting on the center thwart, and lying down on the canoe's bottom.

Reentry into the canoe is accomplished by reaching across the canoe (amidships) to the far-side gunwale, and with a vigorous flutter kick and pull by the arms, bring the chest and thighs across the near-side gunwale. A flip of the body and turn puts you in a sitting position inside the canoe. Bring the legs inside, move to your seat, and resume paddling.

Try swamping the canoe or tip it over, then

*The smallest canoe available is Old Town's Pack Canoe, slightly over 10′ long, and weighing 18 pounds.*

hang on to the sides to prove to yourself that, even when completely filled with water, or upside-down, the canoe will not sink.

Somewhere in practicing these get-acquainted activities, swim while fully clothed to learn how your floating and swimming skills are impaired. Practice taking off your shoes and clothes while treading water, and swim to shore. (Note: This is a learning procedure, and in an actual canoeing situation, you would rarely leave an upset canoe. You have verified that a completely swamped canoe will float and in effect serve as an effective life preserver in its own right.)

Alternately and repeatedly, you and your buddy should experience the above procedures, and soon, satisfactory skills and confidence will emerge.

## SPECIALIZED USES OF THE CANOE

You are now ready for more extensive activities. Don't allow inexperience to hold you back. The versatile nature of the canoe enables you to use it in many ways: poling, sailing, rowing, and motorboating.

**Poling** There are many waters with swift currents, or with narrow passages and many

*Canoeing on emerald waters, with Victoria Glacier in the background (Canadian Government Travel Bureau Photo).*

boulders that can be negotiated best with the use of a pole. This aspect of the canoeman's art involves braking and propulsion techniques much more effective than a paddle's.

The pole as a piece of equipment is rarely carried in the canoe, but is picked up as needed. It should be 10' to 12' long and approximately 1½" in diameter. The pole is shod with an iron spike, attached by means of a cap fitting over the end of the pole and anchored with a nail or screw. The shod is carried as a piece of equipment, ready for use when needed.

The only time the canoeist should stand in a canoe is when he is using the pole. The technique calls for standing forward of the stern seat with your feet apart in a stable stance, the left foot forward of the right, both toed in, so that (as a right-handed canoeist) you're facing and leaning slightly to the starboard poling side. After about 10 minutes of practice, you will have learned much about body balance and canoe response.

Select a shallow, quiet section of water for your initial attempts in poling, then work up to a shallow stream where you have boulders, sandbars, and a current to contend with.

**Sailing**  The canoe is easily rigged up for sailing. The single lateen sailing rig is most popular and can be raised in minutes. The lateen sail consists of a nearly equilateral triangular cloth attached to 2 spars linked together at a meeting point forward of the mast.

Whether you buy a sailing rig or build your own depends on time, economy, and your skill as a craftsman. The major canoe companies have "tailor-made" sailing accessories to fit their models. Utilizing adapters, clips, wing nuts, clamps, etc., they are engineered for quick attachment and detachment.

The canoe under sail will run well, point high on a windward course, come about easily, and give a fast ride. For your first experience in sailing, select a wide stretch of water, not subject to squalls and without dangerous currents or obstructions.

**Rowing** The canoe can be converted into a racing shell, a young person's rowing trainer, or a high-speed life-saving or emergency craft for the camp waterfront. The attachment required consists of metal oarlock arms, sliding seat, adjustable foot blocks, and spoon-blade racing oars. The rowing rig is easily attached to a canoe by means of 4 clamps and wing nuts. No tools are needed, and installation time is only a few minutes. The rig combines the maneuverability

*A rowing rig is easily attached to this 16′ Old Town canoe.*

and carrying capacity of a rowboat and some of the speed of a racing shell.

Young men and women are especially partial to the rig, which offers competition speed propulsion. The rowing rig also gives novices confidence in canoe handling. Their durability makes them feasible for enabling enthusiasts to get racing shell experience without going to the expense of buying a real shell.

**Motorboating** A small outboard motor effectively moves the canoe for more than 5 hours on a gallon of gas. Although canoeing purists reject the use of an outboard, for canoeists not conditioned physically, those who do not wish to backtrack a long route by paddling, and those whose time is limited, the outboard, to quickly push along the canoe, is the answer. And in emergency situations, the outboard can save lives.

The canoeist should keep in mind that a heavy motor on a small canoe will adversely affect its trim, balance, freeboard, and stability. Speed should rarely be the sole justification for the outboard. For better economy in fuel consumption, observation advantages, and safety factors, the motor should rarely be driven "wide open."

A combination of paddling and outboarding

# DO'S & DON'TS FOR CANOE & KAYAK

DO WEAR AN APPROVED LIFE JACKET WHEREVER UPSETS MAY OCCUR – A CRASH HELMET IS RECOMMENDED FOR WHITEWATER (life jacket must be capable of supporting you face up)

DON'T BOAT ALONE, EXCEPT ON SMALL QUIET LAKES AND CALM SLOW-MOVING RIVERS (have an observer on shore)

DO KEEP CLEAR OF OTHER CRAFT (you may have the right of way but they probably can't see you)

DON'T CHANGE PLACES OR STAND UP IN A MOVING CANOE OR KAYAK

DO equip your boat with safety devices (Spare paddle --- Bow & stern lines, securely attached to boat, coiled neatly and secured for quick release --- Adequate flotation in bow and stern --- Floating flashlight or battery lantern in case darkness sneaks up on you).
    DON'T paddle beyond a returnable distance from start (always let someone know where you are going and when you think you will return).

DO test all new and unfamiliar equipment before taking chances.
    DON'T attempt waters beyond your ability (have a frank knowledge of your boating skills).

DO ask about local conditions; tides, currents, rapids and weather conditions (they can be tricky or dangerous).
    DON'T wear heavy boots or jackets (you can't swim in heavy clothing).

DO keep away from weirs and dams --- they're dangerous.
    DON'T forget --- better safe than sorry.

DO travel in a group, wherever possible --- it's more fun.
    DON'T be put off by this list --- it's all common sense.

DON'T CANOE IF YOU CAN'T SWIM (be a competent swimmer with ability to handle yourself under water)

DO BE SURE YOUR CRAFT IS IN GOOD REPAIR BEFORE SETTING OUT (always carry a patch kit for emergency repairs)

DON'T PUT MORE PEOPLE IN A CANOE OR KAYAK THAN IT IS DESIGNED TO CARRY

DO STAY WITH A CAPSIZED CANOE OR KAYAK – HANG ON (it may float & you may not)

offers the ideal arrangement. Canoeists who are sensitive to the outdoors will understand when to paddle and when to use the outboard.

### AREAS OF USE

Most of us yearn to escape from living in one truly disadvantaged area—the big city. Man has a need for solitude and, with the canoe, escape from frenzied schedules, crowded places, and loud noises, is possible around the bend of a local river, slowly cruising between soft banks as if you were a thousand miles from home.

With the resurgence of canoeing, paddlers are rediscovering many streams once believed to have little interest to them. A few of them, along with others recently in the news are listed: recently opened canoe trails in the Everglades National

Park in Florida and the Okefenokee Wilderness in Georgia; the old canals, such as the Illinois-Michigan Canal in Illinois and the Erie Canal in New York; the remote and calm waters of Zane Grey country in Canyonlands National Park, Utah; Shoshone and Yellowstone Lakes in Yellowstone National Park; portions of the mountain valley rivers of Wyoming and Colorado; the salt marshes, isolated sloughs, and tidal flats of San Francisco Bay; and Alaskan rivers, which offer hundreds of miles of cruising without portages. And, if you hanker to ply the mighty Mississippi, the U.S. Corps of Engineers, 906 Oliver St., St. Louis, Missouri, 63102, offers river charts and facilities for various sectors of the river. This list, of necessity, is brief. A letter to the conservation department of the state or province in Canada of your interest will bring further information on canoe trails.

*Youth hostel's canoers take a lunch break on the banks of the Des Plaines River in Illinois.*

(Note: The results of the most extensive search for canoe trails in the United States and Canada are contained in *Malo's Complete Guide to Canoeing and Canoe-Camping.*)

## LOCAL USES

The canoe is easily transported, and if water is anywhere close to home, you can car-top your canoe for leisurely cruising, sailing, hunting, or fishing, at any time of the day or evening.

**Hunting** The canoe offers hunting areas that are ignored or inaccessible by other craft. Take to the wetlands that are too marshy to attract waterfront developers, the back streams that are unreachable by road, and the shallow streams that dissuade the motorboat owner. Surprisingly, there's often no need to travel far, as many prolific hunting grounds can be found close to home. The canoe serves as a means of transportation and, properly camouflaged, as a blind too. Jump shooting of ducks on small streams, protected from high winds and devoid of other hunters, can be highly productive. Migratory waterfowl spend their nights on streams, so an early morning hunt is advised. Late afternoon, when the birds begin to drift in, is another good time.

**Fishing** The float fishing trip offers an ideal way to cover a lot of water, with little disturbance. "Take in" at some country road bridge, and arrange to have one car at the downstream "take out" point. A pushpole may help the stern paddler to negotiate shallow rocky streams, while the bowman uses the conventional paddle. Snubbing with the pole to stop the canoe above likely looking pools, and working the lure at various levels should decoy smallmouth bass and trout. Fish the undercut banks and along heavily covered shorelines with a fast retrieve, especially with a darting spoon or spinner. Fly fishing from the canoe gives adequate back-cast distance and prevents hang-ups.

While floating the meandering stream, you'll be involved as much with the view around each bend as you will with the choice of casting lure. Estimate your floating speed at about 3 mph when considering the schedule of your take-out time. If a large lake, for extensive hunting or fishing, is planned, you should consider pontoons or outriggers to increase stability.

*The float fishing trip offers an ideal way to cover a lot of water—and catch a smallmouth bass.*

## WILDERNESS CANOEING

If you are the type of canoeist whose "thing" is plying the rivers that shout and roar and bellow, then seek out the mountain rivers of the Rockies, the whitewater streams in all parts of Canada and in Michigan, Wisconsin, Minnesota, and Maine. There the restraining riverbanks of granite, along with land declivity, sluice the water in roller coaster runs and the river responds

*Carrying a canoe around the water turbulence of the Berens River in Ontario, Canada*

almost like some digestive tract, convulsing to eliminate an irritating object—your canoe.

All is not fury, however, on the wilderness rivers; most of the way they sound more like Angelus bells or the songs of Finlandia. In the wilderness, the canoeist identifies best with the Indian and his craft: getting closer to nature, causing no harm (pollution) to the land or water, reaching a destination on your own power, using the upturned canoe for shelter in a sudden squall, and carrying it around water turbulence.

A wilderness experience brings one face to face with traditions of primeval kinship, that of relating to the sun, sky, water, trees, and cleanliness—cleanliness everywhere. The wilderness is the last refuge from mechanization, skyscraper horizons, and discordant sounds. Noise pollution is replaced by the piping of a shore bird, the thrum of a frog, and the laughter of a loon.

For additional information contact the American Canoe Association, 400 Eastern St., New Haven, Connecticut, 06513, for local, national and international news of recreational canoeing and canoe sport—in kayak or canoe—on flatwater, flowing river and whitewater, equipment

news, canoe camping ideas, schedules of events, etc. The entire scope of wilderness adventuring is contained in *Wilderness Canoeing* (New York: The Macmillan Company, 1971).

### THE CANOE AND ECOLOGY

The canoe represents a non-polluting craft supreme. An excellent example is shown by the Annual Des Plaines River Canoe Marathon (approximately 8 miles west of Chicago, Illinois city limits), sponsored by the Illinois Paddling Council.

Since its inception in 1958, the marathon has burgeoned into the largest single canoe event on the continent. Under the leadership of Ralph Frese and Ralph Nelson, in May, 1971, the event attracted 1,201 paddlers in 617 craft which plied the 20-odd mile course from Libertyville to Dam No. 2. As in former marathons, an hour after the last canoe was off the water, an inspection of the entire course showed NO evidence at all that such a magnitude of craft, men, women, and children had used the river.

Individuals, too, can engage in vigorous campaigns to safeguard our waters. The famed "Fox," a type of pollution-fighting Robin Hood in Du-Page County, Illinois, uses the canoe to seek out polluting discharges by factories, packing houses, mills, etc. Completely unidentified, the "Fox," mostly in the cover of darkness, and has cemented the openings of offensive sewers, and has collected various forms of polluting material in plastic bags, and dumped them in the corridors and offices of offending companies.

Three pollution bounty hunters in Pittsburgh, Pennsylvania, stalked by canoe for 3 months to establish a river-polluting charge against a chemical corporation. They were awarded $5,000 for the evidence that led to conviction by a federal judge. The sum was equal to half of the $10,000 fine, and stemmed from the 1899 Rivers and Harbors Act, which states that the government will split 50-50 with whomever provides the evidence.

Of all the groups using off-road vehicles or craft, the canoeists need least an image building project, yet they are in the forefront of most stream clean-up campaigns throughout the country. They realize that their water heritage must be zealously guarded. Should the river in your area need a clean-up, Grumman (see Buyer's Guide) offers a free brochure, "How to Organize Your Waterway Clean-Up by Canoe." Some water guidelines follow:

1. Be ever vigilant for misuse, pollution, and littering of waterways.

2. Send water samples to the local or state anti-pollution board.

3. Publicize the findings through all possible news media.

4. Involve the local citizenry, conservation groups, and scout groups in establishing a broad base of support.

5. Apprise landowners contiguous to the water-way of their particular benefits that accrue from a clean river in property and esthetic values.

6. With solid evidence and support of many, take the case to your elected officials and hound them to action.

## BUYER'S GUIDE

Present-day canoes seem to be associated with established companies by their type of construction: Grumman, aluminum; Old Town, wood-canvas; and Trailcraft, fiberglass.

Your choice of a canoe should depend upon the intended use, type of water, and extent of participation. No prices are quoted, but some general guidelines follow:

The 18' size aluminum and fiberglass models sell for approximately $285. The wood-canvas models are approximately $310. In computing the price of other sizes of the double-end canoe, add approximately $15 for each additional foot of length or deduct approximately $15 for each foot less than the 18' size. Manufacturers include:

Berry Boats, Waitsfield, Vermont, 05073

Chestnut, Moor and Mountain, 14 Main St., Concord, Massachusetts, 01742 (Canadian-built canoes)

Cloudcap Chalet, 625 S.W. 12 Ave., Portland, Oregon, 97205

Core Craft, Bemidji Boat Co., Highway 2 West, Bemidji, Minnesota, 56601

Dutch Craft Co., 1421 Bay St. S.E., St. Petersburg, Florida, 33701

Edo Western Corp., 2645 S. 2nd West, Salt Lake City, Utah, 84115

Grumman Boats, Marathon, New York, 13803

Mohawk, Box 668, Longwood, Florida, 32750

Old Town Canoe Co, Old Town, Maine, 04468

Ouachita Marine, Box 420, Arkadelphia, Arkansas, 71923

Richland Mfg, Box 508, Richland, Missouri, 65556

Sawyer Canoe Co., 234 S. State St., Oscoda, Michigan, 48750

Sportsal, Drawer T, Emlenton, Pennsylvania, 16373

Trailcraft, Box 60680, Concordia, Kansas, 66901

# APPENDIX

## ALL-TERRAIN VEHICLE ASSOCIATIONS

National All-Terrain Vehicle Assoc., 324 Broad St., New Bethlehem, Pennsylvania, 16242

National Off-Road Racing Assoc., 1616 Victory Blvd., Glendale, California, 91201

Canadian All-Terrain Vehicle Mfgers. Assoc., 161 Orenda Road, Brampton, Ontario, Canada

## CANOEING ASSOCIATIONS

American Canoe Assoc., 400 Eastern St., New Haven, Connecticut, 06513

American Whitewater Club, 1925 Hopkins St., Berkeley, California, 94707

American Red Cross: contact your local chapter

American Youth Hostels, 20 W. 17th St., New York, New York, 10011

United States Canoe Assoc., 6338 Hoover Road, Indianapolis, Indiana, 46260

Wisconsin Hoofers Club, Memorial Union, Univ. of Wisconsin, Madison, Wisconsin, 53706

Canadian Canoe Assoc., 3212 St. Joseph Blvd., Lachine, Quebec, Canada

## DUNE BUGGY ASSOCIATIONS

### Far West

Baja Racing Assoc., Box 1803, Calexico, California, 92231

CORVA, 8612 Boyson St., Downey, California, 90242

John Jones, 4806 Market St., San Diego, California, 92102

Palm Springs Dune Buggy Assoc., Box 931, Palm Springs, California, 92662

### West

Phoenix 4-Wheelers, Box 15412, Phoenix, Arizona, 85018

Gene Graves, 310 Morgan St., Truth or Consequences, New Mexico, 87901

### Midwest

MORCA, 913 W. Lake St., Minneapolis, Minnesota, 55408

Ogema Sport & Trail Center, Box 117, Rose City, Michigan, 48654

### East

Aces Car Club Assoc., Box 2432, Trenton, New Jersey, 08607

Eastern Dune Buggy Assoc., Box 3261, Orlando, Florida, 32802

Indian River Dune Runners, Box 1054, Ft. Pierce, Florida, 33450

## DUNE BUGGY PUBLICATIONS

Dune Buggies & Hot VWs, Box 1757, Newport Beach, California, 92663

4 × 4 Dunebuggy News, Box 5001, Mission Hills, California, 91340

Road Test Dunebuggy, Box 22018, Los Angeles, California, 90022

## FOUR-WHEEL DRIVE VEHICLE ASSOCIATIONS

National 4-WD Association, Box 12798, Seattle, Washington, 98146, or 936 Ireland Ave., Muskegon, Michigan, 49441

National Jeep Clubs, 40 N. Cone Blvd., Toledo, Ohio, 43601

## FOUR-WHEEL DRIVE PUBLICATIONS

Four Wheeler Magazine, 1680 N. Vine St., Hollywood, California, 90028

Off-Road Vehicles Magazine, 131 S. Barrington Place, Los Angeles, California, 90049

Sand N' Street News, Box 2336, Pleasant Hill, California, 94523

## MOTORBIKE ASSOCIATIONS

American Motorcycle Assoc., 5655 N. High St., Worthington, Ohio, 43085

## MOTORBIKE PUBLICATIONS

Popular Cycling, and Minibike Yearbook, 131 S. Barrington Pl., Los Angeles, California, 90049

Minibike World, 1499 Monrovia Ave., Newport Beach, California, 92663

Track & Trail, 1999 Shapard Road, St. Paul, Minnesota, 55116

Minibike Guide, 2420 Wilshire Blvd., Santa Monica, California, 90403

Guide to Safe Motorcycling, American Automobile Assoc., 1712 G St., Washington, D.C., 20006

## SNOWMOBILE ASSOCIATIONS

### General

American Snowmobile Assoc., Box Columbia Hights, 4403, Minneapolis, Minnesota, 55403

United States Snowmobile Assoc., 101 Snowmobile Drive, Eagle River, Wisconsin, 54521

International Snowmobile Industry Assoc., 734 15th St. N.W., Washington, D.C., 20005

### West

Rocky Mountain Snowmobile Assoc., Box 323, Frisco, Colorado, 80443

Western Snowmobile Assoc., 610 Idaho St., Boise, Idaho, 83702

### Midwest

International Snowmobile Assoc., 9 E. Harvey St., Ely, Minnesota, 55731

Michigan Snowmobile Assoc., 229 W. 15th St., Traverse City, Michigan, 49684

North Central Assoc., 2901 Pleasant Ave., Minneapolis, Minnesota, 55408

### East

Adirondack Snowmobile Assoc., Lake Pleasant, New York, 12108

Snowmobile Council of Massachusetts, Westfield, Massachusetts, 01085

Maine Snowmobile Assoc., Box 88, East Winthrop, Maine, 04343

North American Snowmobile Assoc., 18 School St., Concord, New Hampshire, 03301

New Hampshire Snowmobile Assoc., Box 643, Manchester, New Hampshire, 03105

Vermont Assoc. of Snow Travelers, Box 839, Montpelier, Vermont, 05602

### Canada

Canadian Snowmobile Assoc., 38 Vincent, Ste. Agathe Des-Monts, Quebec, Canada

Ontario Federation of Snowmobile Clubs, 208 Ring St., Toronto, Canada